Baby Shower Fun

by

Sharon Dlugosch
with
ShowerWise

BRIGHTON PUBLICATIONS, INC.

Illustrations By Sandra Knuth

BRIGHTON PUBLICATIONS, INC.

Copyright © 1987 by Sharon E. Dlugosch

Brighton Publications, Inc.
P.O. Box 12706
New Brighton, MN 55112
(612) 636-2220

First Edition: 1987

Printed in the United States of America
Library of Congress Catalog
Card Number: 83-072953
International Standard Book Number:
0-918420-14-8

CONTENTS

ShowerWise Gift Themes / 63

ShowerWise Sprinkles / 69

ShowerWise Steps / 78

ShowerWise Guides / 86

Before the Beginning . . .

T his book was written because I always thought showers were boring. I tried to be pleasant and hide this fact, but then on one bright and sunny day someone finally said it—(it could have been me) "I HATE SHOWERS!"

Having faced the fact that showers were at best "have to" parties that I had to either attend or give, I realized there must be other people who felt the same way. Without any effort at all, I found other closet shower haters.

Well, believe it or not, this was the beginning of the Baby Shower Fun book! I've learned several interesting bits of information in talking with many women and from the results of a shower survey I mailed to individuals and gift stores around the country. Even though people were tired of giving and going to the same, old, worn-out showers, no one wanted to give up the idea completely.

This presented a real problem, because, before the results of the shower survey came in, I had decided that giving showers was a thing of the past. But after giving it some thought, I realized what most of us were really experiencing. Busy schedules, limited funds, wanting to include husbands and fathers, and not knowing how to put on a really fun, memorable shower were all part of the uneasiness about showers.

Perhaps now I could begin to find an answer. Showers are still "in," I decided, but the times have changed. Baby showers have to change to accommodate the busy lifestyles of women today, the growing trend of showers for couples, and the desire of friends and relatives to share in making memories for the new parents.

"What I really need now," I said as I sat down at my word processor, "is someone who has been in the baby business for quite some time." Just then, as if on cue, a quite trim and tidy looking stork popped her head into my window. With a flip of her wing, she bowed and said, "ShowerWise is my name – fond memories, my game!" Could it be? Could this be the help I was looking for?

"You're on the right flight pattern," she said, dancing a little two-step. "Baby showers today can truly be fun parties that create memories for the party giver and guest alike."

Trying hard to look composed, I nodded my head in agreement.

"Guests shouldn't have to just sit at the shower looking at the guest of honor opening her gifts. Plan the kind of shower that will make it fun and worthwhile for the guests to attend as well as the guest of honor. Create curiosity and enthusiasm about your shower theme to get people to the shower, and once they're there reward them with special activities and attractions. If you can't get the guests or guest of honor to the shower because of busy schedules, then bring the shower to them and work it into the day's activities."

Crossing one bony leg over the other, she said, "In other words, you have to zig a little when people expect you to zag."

Trying to look wise as I said this, "I get it! You're saying shower planning should involve first-class flights of fancy. The unexpected activity, location, or invitation can bring the baby shower to new heights of party-giving."

"Yes, yes, that's all true," she said impatiently "But don't forget that the party giver should have fun at the party, too. Throwing a baby shower shouldn't bankrupt your budget or your energy."

"Well then, it seems to me that we should plan baby showers that are fun and easy for ourselves as well as for our guests."

"You said we!" she shouted while skipping about and preening her feathers. "Does this mean we're going to be working together?"

"Well, with your intimate knowledge of babies and new parents and the shower ideas I collected from the survey," I said as I tried to match her dancing steps, "I think we would make a great team!"

As you can guess, we did go on to create baby shower themes. You'll find they are fun, easy, and just for you, from ShowerWise and . . .

Sharon Dlugosch

Dear ShowerWise

W hat kinds of shower problems are of the most concern today? Well, busy schedules, limited funds, the trend to include fathers, and a desire to give a fun, imaginative shower were most often mentioned in my shower survey . . . all questions that needed answers!

Without hesitation, I turned to ShowerWise. Could she find some answers? Could she ever! Quick as a wink she came up with interesting and in some cases, surprising, answers. (I knew she would.)

It's all here for you. Simply find the questions that are meaningful to you and read the suggested shower helps found in each answer. You'll be glad you did.

Dear ShowerWise,

I'm not into silly games or superficial conversation. I want my guests to feel that any time they spend at my shower is time well spent. Do you have some creative shower ideas for someone like me?

— Down With Games

Dear Down With Games,

We had you in mind when we created this book. The emphasis is on activities. You'll find fifty shower themes and sprinkles packed with quality ideas. Two themes fit your requirements especially well. Solve the Mystery Shower will challenge your guests' power of deduction and Lullaby Time Shower will have your guests recording their favorite rendition of a childhood song or rhyme for the new baby's lullaby tape.

Dear ShowerWise,

My intentions are good, but a look at my budget precludes any large shower doings. I suspect my friends are in the same situation.

— Limited In Funds

Dear Limited In Funds,

There's no need to skip a shower because of a lack of funds. You can sidestep expensive gifts and elaborate entertaining with imaginative shower ideas. The "IOU" shower invites guests to give gifts of personal promises of a service that can be called on at any time. These kinds of gifts can't be bought with dollars. Our Next-To-New Shower is keyed to low budgets as well. It shares food costs with a potluck supper, and only hand-me-downs or secondhand finds are allowed as gifts.

Dear ShowerWise,

Don't get me wrong . . . I'm quite happy with the way I've been doing showers. And yet . . . I would like to think up a clever twist to the shower theme.

– Almost Satisfied

Dear Almost Satisfied,

We have just the thing for you. Put the emphasis on gift-giving with our ShowerWise Gift Theme ideas. It's a way of adding a bit of spice to the occasion. Or borrow decorating and gift ideas from Balloon Shower. It's a fun-filled, "get-happy" theme.

Dear ShowerWise,

This may seem somewhat unusual, but I would like to shower a first-time grandmother. Is this proper?

– Concerned

Dear Concerned,

Not only is the idea of showering the new grandmother thoughtful and delightful, it makes just plain ordinary sense! What grandmother today doesn't need the basic paraphernalia when baby comes to visit? Besides, a shower will allow Grandma to share her excitement and happiness with her friends. Turn to our First-Time Grandmother Shower immediately. Don't stop . . . advance to go . . . and collect raves and applause.

Dear ShowerWise,

Giving a shower is no problem for me. Getting people to come has always been my big headache. Is there a secret?

– Give Me A Clue

Dear Give Me A Clue,

No secret, just some sneaky motivation. The more enthusiasm and fun you can muster in your invitation, the more likely people will be to drop everything to come. Clever and informal invitations are the rule today, and you'll find all kinds of those ideas in our Invitations Guide.

Dear ShowerWise,

As friends of both the new mom and dad, we don't want to leave out Dad at this baby shower. What to do?
– Friendly Dilemma

Dear Friendly Dilemma,

Your feelings are shared by many. Since new fathers today are asked to play a larger part in child rearing, it seems kind of silly to leave them out of the baby shower ritual. By all means plan to give a couples shower. There are several shower themes to choose from that will be fun for a mixed crowd. We especially like the Baby Brunch Shower and the Solve the Mystery Shower.

Dear ShowerWise,

Our group wants to do something more for this baby shower rather then simply bring gifts that may be duplicated. Any ideas for a concentrated group effort?
– More Is Better

Dear More Is Better,

Right off the top of our heads we can mention three ideas that call for a group effort with a unique, personalized gift as the end result. Check out the Decorating Baby's Room Shower, the Quilting Bee Shower and Baby Stitchery Shower. All of these take a bit of planning and coordination but are well worth the time and effort.

Dear ShowerWise,
Honestly, if I have to give another baby shower where everyone sits and looks at each other, I'll soon come unhinged. There must be an alternative!
– Not Quite Unhinged

Dear Not Quite Unhinged,
There's no need to lose your screws yet. All you need is a handy fix-up shower blueprint that will get everyone involved. Arrange a how-to session at your shower, such as balloon sculpturing, from the Balloon Shower, or choose themes that will help guests learn new things about themselves, such as our Sun Sign and Handwriting Analysis showers. The formula is simple . . . involvement equals fun and good times.

Dear ShowerWise,
We have dear friends who made a sudden career move out of state. Time wasn't available to shower them before the move, but now we're thinking about having a long-distance shower. Are we being unrealistic?
– Caring Friends

Dear Caring Friends,
Friends like you make the world go 'round. You can still shower your friends and make the miles apart seem shorter to boot. Just turn to our Special Delivery Shower for an extraordinary shower idea that will make this event a memorable one for everyone.

Dear ShowerWise,
I know at least two other people who are going to shower a popular new mother. How can I make sure she won't receive duplicate gifts?
– Multiple Gifts

Dear Multiple Gifts,

Gently steer her to the baby registry at her favorite store. Our Baby Registry Shower solves the gift-giving dilemma and makes gift-opening time a lot more fun with a gift charades game. Try a different approach with our Baby How-To Shower. Here the new mother is showered with gifts of personal tips and advice on how to take care of baby. You'll find these gifts will be hard to duplicate.

Dear ShowerWise,

I was doing just fine in planning a baby shower for my friend until I heard the news . . . twins! This has to be a great shower now!

— Doubly Delighted

Dear Doubly Delighted,

We agree, the news of twins is always a day brightener. Mark the occasion with our special, "It's Twins!" Shower. You'll find a unique invitation verse, decorations, party-favor ideas, and a guessing game activity just right for this twin event!

Dear ShowerWise,

I'm tired of rushing about when giving a party and not really enjoying any of the fun. Everything must be under control so I can enjoy the shower, too.

— Too Busy To Enjoy

Dear Too Busy To Enjoy,

Make a promise to yourself that this time is going to be different. Choose a shower theme like our Make-Ahead Shower, where everything is done beforehand and party time is spent with your guests. Another choice is to follow a co-hostess plan, as in the Second-Time-Around Shower. It's always a good idea to share entertaining duties with others, giving you time to get in on some of the fun, too. A good rule of thumb is to pick an easy theme you'll feel comfortable with and simplify . . . simplify . . . simplify!

Dear ShowerWise,
   My friend has been through some difficult times and I want her to feel special and pampered at this shower.
                                                        – Searching

Dear Searching,
   Treat your friend to some royal shower giving with the Queen for a Day Shower. Do it up right and she'll feel like royalty for a long time. Or, if your friend has been house bound, she'll especially appreciate the atmosphere of a good restaurant, as in the Second-Time-Around Shower.

Dear ShowerWise,
   I have my baby shower planned except for one last detail. I want a snazzy but easy dessert idea that carries out the baby shower theme.
                                                        – Well Prepared

Dear Well Prepared,
   In our Recipe Guide we have several wonderful recipes that carry out the baby shower theme. But a drop-dead dessert idea we think you'll be especially pleased with is the Cream Puff Pram recipe. It's a can't-fail dessert that will raise plenty of oohs and ahhs!

Dear ShowerWise,
   I've just agreed to be a co-hostess at a baby shower. This may be hard to believe, but I've never attended a shower. What does one do at such an event?
                                                        – Perplexed

Dear Perplexed,

It's really quite simple. Friends and relatives come together to shower the new mother, and dad too, as the case may be. The hard part is making sure everyone has a good time. For a blow-by-blow account, read over our theme for The Basic Shower. From there, look over the other ShowerWise themes, gift themes, and sprinkles, and match a theme to your guest list. You'll see that you have quite a variety of plans to choose from.

Dear ShowerWise,

You don't have to give me the whole picture. Just give me the start of an idea and I'll take it from there.

– Easily Creative

Dear Easily Creative,

There are twenty-five idea starters waiting for you in our ShowerWise Sprinkles section. Not complete themes . . . just odds and ends to help you get started in planning your own personalized and individual shower. Now, get ready . . . set . . . go!

Dear ShowerWise,

It's the first grandchild on either side of the family. I'd like to invite both sides to my shower, but how can I make it fun and interesting for everyone?

– Anxious

Dear Anxious,

We have a tailor-made shower plan for a thoughtful relative such as you. The trick is to give equal time to both sides of the family. Check out the ideas in our Family-Style Shower theme. We think everyone will have fun and at the same time get to know each other a little bit better.

Dear ShowerWise,
Help! My shower is planned for sometime in December. How do I make my shower a standout when the holiday rush is on?

—December Blues

Dear December Blues,
Borrow from the holiday and create a theme that reflects the Christmas spirit, like our The Littlest Angel Shower. This theme allows you to take advantage of your holiday-decorated home, so you only need to decorate once. You'll find several bright ideas in our ShowerWise Sprinkles for other times of the year too.

Dear ShowerWise,
Wouldn't you know it! This seems to be the very busiest time of year. How can I get everyone together to shower our friend?

—Squeezed For Time

Dear Squeezed For Time,
Since time is limited, pack up a Bag a Lunch Shower and bring the shower to your friends. This shower theme is comfortable in any setting, whether classroom, exercise room or church meeting room. Too short a workday to shower a co-worker? Then turn to our easy Office Shower theme. Everyone can enjoy the shower while eating a quick lunch.

Dear ShowerWise,
I owe my friend a shower, but I'm fresh out of decorating and activity ideas.

—Bankrupt

Dear Bankrupt,

It's easy to turn a debt into a dividend with a new source of ideas. After browsing through Themes and Sprinkles, turn to our eleven ShowerWise Guides. You'll find great decorating and activity ideas as well as plenty of other helps to get you started on a shower that will be a pleasure to repay.

ShowerWise Themes

If there's one thing we've heard more often than not, it's the lament, "Spare me from one more boring shower!" Well, ShowerWise says, "There's no need for boring showers. One sure thing to remember when planning a shower is . . . guests start to enjoy themselves when they get involved!"

Since ShowerWise felt strongly about this sense of involvement, we have focused our shower theme planning primarily on activities. We did, however, add clever and unique recipes, decorations, and gift and invitation ideas as well. Only a few game ideas are given here because a collection of games and game sheets can be found in our separate publication, *Games For Baby Shower Fun* (Available at the same fine stores as this book or write to Brighton Publications, Inc. See Address Guide.).

You'll find that the activities we've included will have your guests contributing their time, talents, or labor. Whether lighthearted or heavy-duty, these activities demand involvement. Then, too, you'll see how well-planned activities will help your guests become acquainted, give them something to do, and keep conversation flowing.

Our shower themes give you the option of women-only or couples showers . . . at-home showers or showers at a fellowship hall and picnic area . . . showers timed for an hour in the office day or fitted into the exercise class schedule. Whatever the choice, the greater the sense of involvement you can give each guest who attends, the more successful the shower will be.

Oh yes, one more thing. ShowerWise wants to make sure you understand that you can mix and match theme ideas to create your own custom-made theme shower. Also, if you like a theme idea for a couples shower, you can adapt the idea for a couples group, for women only, or for a family.

Now relax . . . take your time . . . and look through all the themes, sprinkles, and guides. Then choose the ideas that will help make your shower a fun occasion where everyone can have an enjoyable time!

The Basic Shower

Planning a baby shower, especially if it is a first-time attempt, can be an unsettling experience. This shower theme is meant to take you by the hand and walk you through the steps of a shower, beginning with invitations and ending with refreshments. Once you know the basics, you can go on to add imaginative touches that will make your shower sparkle with excitement. So for you first-timers and anyone else who is curious, this basic shower theme is for you.

The basic parts of a shower are invitations, decorations, activities, gift opening, and refreshments. Once you're familiar with the basics, you can page through this book and choose

from a selection of activities, decorations, and so on that will
fit your style of entertaining. You will see how all or some of
the parts can help emphasize any special theme you might
choose for your shower. Don't overlook the Twelve Steps to
a Successful Shower and the Planning Sheet to help you plan
your shower.

Today, since party giving is usually informal, you can start
to have fun right away with eye-catching invitations. This is
an opportunity to share the excitement and fun you expect
to have at your baby shower. Just be sure to do the inviting
at least four or five weeks in advance.

Express your enthusiasm through telephone invitations,
mailed messages, or in-person invitations. You'll be pleased
with the posivitive response if you send attention-grabbing
invitations. Send singing telegrams or give small teddy
bears "bearing" invitations . . . anything that will capture
their attention. (Be sure to see our Invitations Guide for
more sit-up-and-pay-attention ideas.) If you send only a
printed, store-bought invitation, add extra warmth with a
handwritten note under the verse saying something like: "I
hope you can come and share Suzie's happiness with her new
baby!"

When an occasion demands a formal invitation, simply
write the invitation in script on white or cream-colored stationary. It should contain this basic information:

Jane Smith and Mary Anderson
request the pleasure of your company
at a baby shower
for Suzie Michaelson
on May 10
from 7:00 P.M. to 9:00 P.M.
at 151 Rainbow Lane

R.S.V.P.   151 Rainbow Lane
                                 555-5342

However you decide to extend the invitation, remember – a successful shower begins with the extra thought and star quality you give to your invitations.

Decorations add zest to the shower as well. You can't have enough decorations or gimmicks to get everyone into the mood for your shower. Decorate your room or space, table, gift-opening area, or even yourself and your guests. (To see what I mean about decorating your guests, take a look at the Decorations Guide.) Using theme-related decorations heightens interest and adds a festive touch to any baby shower.

The shower itself is divided into three major parts: conversation and/or activity, gift opening and refreshments. The timetable used here is approximately two hours from start to finish. Of course, this can vary depending on the theme and activity chosen or the number of guests at the shower.

SHOWER TIMETABLE

First guest arrives.

First 45 minutes allow time for converstion and/or activity.

Next half hour is given to gift opening (may be part of the activity).

Last 45 minutes are the time for refreshments to be served.

End of shower.

The conversation and/or activity time is often the cause of serious party jitters for the hostess. It is often at this point that a shower stands or falls. Providing a theme with activities involving all the guests will result in everyone's having a good time.

To choose a successful activity, you have to accurately gauge the interest level of all your guests. It goes almost without saying that if the guests are of various ages and backgrounds, you're going to have to spend a little more time thinking up a good theme and activity for all to share. Read all the themes and sprinkles to find an activity exactly suited to your shower and guest list.

As hostess, you are the one who announces the gift-opening time. It's your responsibility to seat the guest of honor and the guests in such a way to make it easy for them to pass the opened gifts to one another. To better help you understand your role as hostess, be sure to read Shower Protocol in the ShowerWise Steps section.

It's refreshment time now, and you're well into hosting a successful shower. Don't get heavy now and find yourself caught up in fancy servings or huge quantities of food. Just choose a simple menu that will enhance the good feeling and festive occasion of your shower. Although many people serve buffet style, you will see other alternatives when paging through the themes.

Plan your menu to accommodate your serving style. For example, when serving a buffet menu, include only fork or finger food. Seating room may be in short supply and guests should not have to juggle a fork and a knife to cut their food.

At the serving table, you'll have another opportunity to emphasize the shower theme with the table cloth, napkins, and centerpiece. Use the traditional paper baby shower decorations, or take a totally different and unique approach to decorating the table. Arrange to have someone dressed as a stork to pour the coffee! See the Decorations and Recipes guides as well as the table blueprints in the Table Setup Guide for ideas to highlight your refreshment area.

This shower theme is meant to give you a bare-bones plan to get you started in planning a shower that is uniquely yours. Pick out a theme, add your enthusiasm and personal touch, and put on the most successful, fun-filled shower of the year. Go to it!

Balloon Shower

Everyone is a kid at heart and this shower should prove to your guests that they are still young enough to get a kick out of a bunch of balloons. Balloons will be the major ingredient of this shower, starting with the invitations and on through the shower until everyone finally reaches the "balloon satiation" point.

Give your friends a hint of what lies ahead with these light-hearted invitation balloons. For each invitation, pick out one medium to large balloon per guest. Don't let yourself get stuck on pink or blue colors; use every color in the rainbow. This is a get-happy shower! Write the invitation information on the balloon with a black marking pen. You will have an easier time of it if you blow up the balloon first, but you can do it either way. If you don't have room for all the information on one balloon, use two balloons. Deflate the balloon and tuck it into an addressed envelope along with a card saying "Please blow me up and read."

Of course, before the shower you're going to decorate with balloons till you bring your guests almost to the point of sensory overload. Tie balloons to the guest of honor's chair, arrange them on the gift table, and fasten them to light fixtures and drapery rods.

Decorate the refreshment table with this balloon centerpiece. Tie together a bunch of small to medium-sized helium-filled balloons and tuck the end of the strings into a brightly colored paper bag. (The bag is going to be the anchor for the balloons.) Tuck tissue paper of contrasting color into the bag around the balloon strings. (See the illustration in Decorate Your Table in Decorations Guide.) Your party supply store will be happy to fill balloons with helium. Just don't fill the balloons too far ahead of time . . . there's a possibility the air will leak out.

At a party or paper-product store, shop for balloon theme paper cups, plates, and napkins to add to the table decorations. You'll find miniature hot-air balloons and personalized balloons there, too.

At the shower, start the festivities with a balloon-sculpturing demonstration. Ask a friend with a large lung capacity who is willing to learn about balloon sculpturing to pass on his or her newfound knowledge at the shower. Or hire someone whose part-time avocation is clowning around. Seriously, you should be able to find a professional clown who would be willing to come and demonstrate for the crowd. By the end of a 30-minute demonstration everyone should have at least one balloon-sculpture favor. Your guests may want to try their hand at balloon sculpture, too. The finished balloons can be donated to the new parents, or the guests can keep them as take-home party favors. After the balloon-sculpting program it's time for gift giving. Guide your guests toward a balloon gift-giving theme and suggest gifts for the baby, such as T-shirts and toddler suits with balloon prints or appliqué, balloon theme nursery lamps, pictures for the nursery, music boxes, and so on. Other gifts can be related to the balloon theme through the gift wrapping. Gift wrap with printed balloon paper, and tie balloons instead of bows to the gift boxes.

And now we're nearing the end of our shower, everyone has had refreshments, and it's time for the last balloon volley. Give each of your guests a slip of paper and have them write a happy wish for the new baby. Then ask them to put the slips in the balloons, blow up the balloons, and release the balloons all together as they are leaving. Pretty, yes, but symbolic too.

There you have it . . . a successful fun-filled – or should I say air-filled – Balloon Baby Shower and you didn't ask your guests, even once, to sit on a balloon and pop it!

Another Idea: Hire a hot-air balloon for rides during the shower . . . that is, if you really want to see your guests get carried away!

Lullaby Time Shower

Remember that favorite lullaby you learned as a child? Tell your friends to be prepared to record their favorite renditions of childhood songs or rhymes at the shower to help create a lullaby tape. They'll be flattered to be asked to share a part of themselves. And it's hard to think of a warmer welcome for baby than the loving voices of Mom and Dad's best friends.

Create the general mood for this venture by including a catchy rhyme with your invitation:

Hey diddle diddle,
Come with your fiddle.
We'll use a little time
To record a song or rhyme!
Bring your favorite lullaby song or rhyme
to record for baby's lullaby tape.

Turn to the Invitations Guide to find a copy of this verse with a printer ready invitation. Just cut it out and take it to a printer.

You may want to add a short note to your invitations suggesting that gifts should tie in with the lullaby time theme. Some good gift ideas are nursery lamps with Mother Goose character bases, rhyme books, nursery rhyme pictures for the wall, clothing, furniture, small rugs and pillows decorated with favorite nursery characters, and mobiles for cribs. A night light and music box are good lullaby-time additions for the nursery too.

Another question, should you be so lucky as to have anyone ask, will be about making up their own rhyme or song. Tell them they'll get four stars if they do. Also they are welcome to add any musical accompaniment to their song or rhyme.

Put "Check recording equipment" and "Buy tapes" on your list of things to do before the shower. It will be worthwhile to have a good- quality tape recorder on hand. Even better, use a microphone with it to pick up every treasured word. Save yourself some time at the party, by making sure there is an outlet handy for the recorder. If you need batteries, check those too, since batteries have a way of wearing down. Guess-timate how many minutes of playing time you'll need and then buy a longer-playing tape if you need it. You can transfer the recording to a shorter tape if you find you overestimated, but at least you'll be sure to have plenty of playing time when you need it.

Now for decorations. You can pull out all the stops and get just as sentimental as you want to with this kind of theme. Decorate the refreshment table with all sorts of lullaby time characters, or choose one rhyme or story. Carry out its theme with colors, cutouts of characters, and a decorated cake centerpiece. You can decorate other strategic areas of your home with characters like Little Miss Muffet, Tom Thumb, the cow who jumped over the moon, and others.

The day of the party is here, most of the guests have arrived, and you're ready to start recording. But first, before you begin, give a few last-minute instructions. To make the tape even more special, ask the group to add their "signature" to the rhyme or song with a simple phrase such as "Aunt Jane loves baby (or name of baby) very much" or "For a beautiful and wonderful baby, with love from Mary". If someone forgot to bring a rhyme or song or couldn't find anything they liked, suggest that they simply say a few happy wishes for the baby, like "You will grow into a warm and loving person" or "Creative and happy thoughts will be yours." Anything can be said, as long as it is positive for the baby. When taping is done, remind the new parents to make a copy of the lullaby tape. If there is time, it would be a nice gesture on your part to make a copy for them during the shower.

After taping, have your guest of honor start opening baby's gifts. Play the completed tape in the background so everyone can share in the creativity and warm wishes. However, be prepared to stop, back up, and replay the tape several times for those who have missed something. When gift opening is finished, invite everyone to the refreshment table, and continue playing the tape if it hasn't finished.

This shower theme provides a fun and creative activity for your guests, while at the same time producing a unique, one-of-a-kind gift that will be treasured always. Who knows, your lullaby time tape may sound so professional you'll want to copyright it!

Baby Brunch Shower

Invite a bunch to a brunch! This combined brunch and baby shower theme lends itself well to a couple's shower. Since it's planned for a mid-morning Saturday or Sunday, everyone can easily come to shower the new parents. Once you get the knack of using a tongue-in-cheek approach to the baby theme, organizing this shower will be easy.

But first, let's get serious about the decorations. Decorate your space with pink and blue ribbons and crepe paper strung across the room or tied in bows. Tape the bows to pictures frames or lampshades. Set small stuffed animals (ducks, lambs, or other baby animals are perfect) on your mantle, bookshelves, or end tables. Tie blue and pink ribbon around the animals' necks and loosely twist the streamers around their legs. Tuck green Easter-basket grass under their feet.

Now turn your attention to the brunch table. Spread a white tablecloth on the table, and drape pink and blue ribbon lengthwise and crosswise on the table. Set a bowl of baby's-breath in the center with tiny pink and blue satin bows tucked among the blossoms. You can find ready-made bows at party-supply companies such as Maid of Scandinavia. You'll find their address in the Address Guide.

Just for fun, substitute baby bibs for napkins at this brunch. Check the newspaper for white sales and buy enough fringed terry cloth hand towels to make a bib for each guest. To make, turn one fringed end of the hand towel over ½ inch and tack down. Run a ¼-inch-wide twill tape through the fold for the bib's tying strings. Finish off the bib with a flourish by writing each guest's name on the bib with a textile marking pen. But wait, this is a baby shower so let's try to use the baby version of each name . . . for example "Bethy" for Beth or "Bry Bry" for Brian.

In keeping with the spirit of this theme, borrow baby bottles (that is, if you don't have your own collection) and pop a straw in each one. These are going to be used as juice glasses during the brunch.

Now for the baby brunch menu. You guessed already from all the foolishness of bibs and baby bottles that this was not going to be an ordinary menu. Highlight the baby brunch shower with a menu that reads like this:

> Humpty Dumpty Egg Bake
> Wee Willie Winkie Wilted Salad
> Three Little Pigs in a Blanket
> Honey Buns

The egg bake is your favorite quiche recipe, the salad is made with Bibb lettuce, and the honey buns are rolls made with honey. You'll find the Three Little Pigs in a Blanket recipe in the Recipes Guide.

In case your guests miss some of the finer points of your menu puns, write the name of each dish in your finest script on place cards. Make out a card for the baby's-breath centerpiece too.

Set your guests in the right frame of mind with unique, wake-up invitations that shout with the news that this is not going to be an ordinary baby shower. Visit the children's section in your local music store. Go through the 45 rpm stack and pull out any records with nursery songs like "Hickory Dickory Dock". You'll need one record for each invitation. Use a marking pen to write the invitation information on the record label, tuck the record between cardboard sheets, and mail to your guests.

At the same time you are choosing your record invitation, look for songs to play as background music for your shower. Greet your guests with the sounds of "It's a Small World" and continue with the soft strains of lullabies.

You can count on this shower to be a real memory-maker for the new parents as well as your guests. So, put away

those frowns and worry lines because this is one shower that
is going to be child's play through and through!

Decorating Baby's Room Shower

Making room for baby becomes a high priority for expectant parents, especially during the last months as the due
date gets closer. This shower is going to help the new mom
and dad ready the baby's nursery, and on time too! Whether
it's a complete paint job or a craft idea that will finish off the
room perfectly, the job will go much faster when good friends
join together.

Before inviting the gang, you'll want to enter high summit
talks with the new parents to decide what projects get the
groon light. Painting and papering walls, laying carpet, or
setting up furniture like baby cribs are all projects the shower group can tackle.

Since this kind of shower theme will probably be picked up
by young friends of the expectant couple who see each other
often, inviting can be rather informal. Just mention the time
and place. Remind them to wear old clothes if the project is
going to be messy.

On the day of the shower, have the game plan pretty well
thought out. Tools and supplies should be in place and a helpful chart listing each step in the project should be nearby.
Have everyone sign up for a task so everyone knows what
to do and can keep on working without getting in each other's
way.

You may decide that the group's time and energy are gift
enough, but if the group would like to bring gifts, too you can
open gifts after everyone has been revived with some
refreshments. Serve "real" food, especially if the project has
involved any kind of physical work. Serve sandwiches made
with thick slices of whole-grain bread, crisp vegetable sticks,
chunky cheese bits, and chooey, gooey cookies and bars for
dessert. Hot coffee, tea or cold juice completes the menu.

Now when everyone's energy has been restored, return to the project area to admire the results of the handiwork while opening gifts. If you made the suggestion to bring gifts specifically for the nursery, each gift can be put in place as soon as it's been passed around the group. Tabletop lamps, crib mobiles, wall pictures, music boxes, grow charts, a baby scale, and a diaper pail would all be welcome additions. As each gift is opened, it can be put in place right away for the final finishing touch. That's why the uniqueness of this shower – that is, being held at the guest of honor's home – works so well.

This shower answers the need to "do something constructive" rather than play games. Everyone is going to go home tired but contented because they played a tangible role in welcoming the new baby!

Another Idea: If the parents are superorganized and have the nursery ready, create some wall decorations as a fun project. Tree Toys, a paper-cutting craft company, has published a parchment paper-snipping nursery rhyme book. The book contains Mother Goose and all the familiar nursery rhyme characters. These can be "snipped" out and mounted on tiny-patterned paper or cloth and framed. If you want to pursue this idea, write to Tree Toys. You'll find them in the Address Guide.

"Sun Sign" Shower

Whether the zodiac chart means anything to you or not, it's fun to exchange astrological signs. After all, the popularity of the horoscope columns should tell us something. Name tags, decorations, and activities will lend themselves easily to the astrological theme of this shower.

Get everyone into the sun sign frame of mind by sending this invitation:

IT'S A LIBRA!

Come to our "SUN SIGN" baby shower!

The Baby's Sun Sign Is _____

Colors: Bright blue and pastels
Flowers: Violet and daffodil
Gem: Opal

FOR:
DATE: TIME:
PLACE:
GIVEN BY:
R.S.V.P.:

P.S.: Please give the month and day of your
birthday with your R.S.V.P.

Keep the invitations and decorations on hold until after the baby has arrived to make sure you're working with the right sun sign. Once you know the date of birth, go to the Decorations Guide and select the sun sign information you need to fill out your invitation. Write or type your invitation on good stationary or baby invitation cards that are blank inside, or see the printer ready invitation in the Invitations Guide. A word of caution: don't ask your guests for the year of their birthday. Some people are sensitive about their age.

Choosing decorations for this sun sign shower will be easy. Use the same colors and flowers as given for baby's sign. If you were to use the sample invitation sun sign, you would use Libra's favorite flowers and colors. For example, you could highlight a centerpiece of African violets with a small card saying "Libra's Preferred Flowers." Complete the decorative theme with ribbons and streamers in Libra's pastel colors. Finally, to draw everyone into the sun sign spirit, Scotch tape each sun sign symbol around the room. Either draw the sun signs or find a zodiac calendar with illustrations of each month's signs.

Once you receive each guest's birth date information, you'll be ready to start on the name tags. Print the name, sun sign, and the names of famous personalities born under the sun sign on a larger-than-normal-sized tag. You can find the famous-personality information in your local library. Look for sun sign pins that can fasten the name tags and be used as party favors as well.

As you're looking for famous personalities for each guest's sun sign, write down any information on their sun sign characteristics. You will be able to use this information for a shower game called "How Well Do You Know the Zodiac?" A multiple-choice format is used because guests who are unfamiliar with astrology will still have a chance to win. Here are some sample questions with answers to get you started.

1) I like to be on top but am still known for being warm-hearted!

Who am I?   Pisces   *Leo*   Capricorn

2) Harmony is my middle name!

Who am I?   *Libra*   Aries   Scorpio

3) I'm protective, especially of the home and family!

Who am I?   Aquarius   Libra   *Cancer*

4) "Me first" is my impulsive cry!

Who am I?   *Aries*   Pisces   Libra

5) I love people—the more the merrier!

Who am I?   Scorpio   *Aquarius*   Capricorn

To get your guests personally involved, ask questions that will touch on the sun sign of each person who is playing the game, then let everyone decide if the sun sign characteristic fits the person. Give an astrology magazine to the person with the most correct answers.

You're sure to be a success with this theme, simply because everyone enjoys learning something new about themselves. Whether we admit to the stars influencing our personalities or not, you can bet Jupiter, the planet of luck, will be shining down on this shower.

Make-Ahead Shower

Plan a simple but elegant make-ahead baby shower around the baby- and-buggy theme. Everything can be done ahead, allowing you plenty of time to relax and enjoy your party. You'll create precious centerpieces, a lovely gift-giving area, and a smashing dessert finale—all with a minimum of time and work.

Add visually to the baby shower theme with groupings of dolls and flowers. You can easily find props from your children's toy chest, or unpack your old favorite baby dolls from your childhood years. You'll serve up a visual treasure if you can unearth a Raggedy Ann and Andy doll set. Prop dolls against the table lamp on the coffee table, or set them by twos back-to-back on the mantle and dessert table. Display cut flowers in children's play teapot sets and pencil boxes, and set them with the doll groupings.

While unpacking your dolls you may come across an old baby buggy. This is just what you need for the gift-giving area. If you don't have an old buggy, borrow a child's toy buggy and spiff it up for its role in the gift-giving area. Tie satin bows and ribbons to the sides and handlebar of the buggy, and line the inside of the carriage with a colorful baby blanket or quilt. As the guests arrive they can place their gifts in and around the buggy.

To highlight the baby-and-buggy theme, serve Cream Puff Prams created by Valyn Love of the Corner Gourmet in

Portland, Oregon. "Pram" is short for "perambulator," the British word for baby buggy. To make this pram, you'll need oval-shaped cream puffs, pastel mints for the wheels, a short pipe cleaner for the pram handle, and a tiny acrylic baby doll to pop into the whipped cream blanket. Love says, "This recipe makes a dessert sweet to see and an edible shower surprise!" See the Recipes Guide for a list of ingredients and directions for these incredible Cream Puff Prams.

Arrange the dessert and beverage in tea-table style on the dessert table. The table may be a dining table, card table, or other small table. Choose decorative paper napkins with a baby shower motif that will complement the baby-and-buggy-theme.

Your step-by-step party plan should include the following:

FOUR OR FIVE WEEKS BEFORE THE SHOWER –
• Send invitations.

THREE DAYS BEFORE THE SHOWER –
• Find dolls, teapot sets and pencil boxes for the decorative groupings.
• Find an old or new buggy and decorate.
• Bake or order cream puffs. (See Recipe Guide for cream puff recipe.)
• Purchase paper napkins.
• Purchase acrylic baby dolls and other ingredients for the Cream Puff Prams.
• Buy paper doilies sized to fit your dessert plates.
• Buy any groceries you may need, coffee, tea, sugar, cream and lemons for slicing.

ONE DAY BEFORE THE SHOWER –
• Place cut flowers in containers and arrange doll groupings.
• Place paper doilies on dessert plates and finishing assembling the Cream Puff Prams. (See Recipe Guide.) Refrigerate.
• Slice lemons. Refrigerate.

- Arrange tablecloth, tableware, and napkins on the dessert table.
- Set the gift buggy in the gift-giving area.

JUST BEFORE THE PARTY –
- Make coffee and hot water for tea. Rinse teapot with hot water.

Lucky you! Now the only thing left to do during the shower is to serve your shower surprise dessert and enjoy! Even cleanup after the party will be minimal because everything was made ahead of time.

This make-ahead shower with its simple but creative party plan will give you can't-fail results. It can be easily hosted by anyone, anyplace!

Second-Time-Around Shower

Simple and easy, this shower takes the once-already mom away from the realities of mothering and whisks her into the world of dress-up clothes, grown-up food and adult conversation. Use a co-hostess plan to share the work and the delight in giving the second-time mom a much-deserved night out at a favorite restaurant or country club. Planning and inviting are shared by co-hostesses, with everyone contributing to the expenses.

You and your co-hostesses will want to meet once to choose a restaurant, decide on the menu, and set the date. At this planning stage add up the expense of the meal, gift, and anything extra such as entertainment. You're going to invite the second-time-around mom as a guest, so include her cost in the budget. As an example, if the meal is $7.50, the gift is $15, and incidentals like flowers and gift wrap are $2.50 per person, ask each guest for $25.00. If a guest cannot attend, offer them the choice of sending a check for the gift only. This way no guest will contribute more than her share.

You can send written invitations, but telephoning is easier and less time-consuming. Divide the list of guests so that each co-hostess has no more than five to ten people to call. Explain the event, time, place, and cost to each guest. You'll probably receive an answer when you call, but if you don't, leave an R.S.V.P. name and number. Encourage the guests to send the donation to you before a set date. This will give you a better head count for making the reservations.

With the gift donation you will be able to buy several small gifts or one large gift that perhaps the guest of honor has openly dreamed about but missed the first time around.

The guest of honor will probably be happy enough with the restaurant surroundings as is, but let's see if we can give a more "showery" touch to the party area. Dress up the table setting with this bright idea . . . a napkin baby bootee! Purchase pastel-colored paper napkins that are at least 16 inches square. Before the day of the shower make up the booties by following the directions under Baby Bootee Napkin Fold in the Decorations Guide. Once you're at the restaurant, set a bootee at each place setting and put mints and nuts or a tiny bouquet of dried flowers in the opening of each bootee. If you wish, prop a name card against each bootee for preplanned seating. Other decorative folded napkins can be found in *Folding Table Napkins*. Write to Brighton Publications, Inc., for ordering information. (See Address Guide.)

If you have bought several small presents, use those along with some flowers as centerpieces at each table or at each section of a large table. The wrapped presents will add color and festivity to each table. When gift-giving time begins, the guest of honor can go to each table to open presents and chat with the guests.

At the table or section where the guest of honor will be seated, place a special take-home centerpiece. Purchase a straw basket with a handle and spray paint it a pretty pastel color. Line the basket with an appropriate baby patterned fabric and paint "FOR BABY" on the handle. Tuck inside a small wrapped present for each member of the family so that no one feels left out of this occasion. Any little ones left at home will be delighted to have a gift, too. The empty basket will make a handy decorative container for the nursery. All in all, perhaps you will agree, this is one of the easy ways to give showers . . . no before-shower housecleaning and no cleanup! This co-hostess planned shower will create an oasis of adult time and elegance for that special mother on her second . . . or third . . . or fourth time around!

Special Delivery Shower

Plan a special delivery of gifts and warm wishes to the absent new parents. If you want to shower the new parents but can't because they live too far away, this theme will make the distance seem shorter. That's right, the new mom and dad are still going to be a part of this shower even though the party's here and they're, well, wherever they are.

For this party, you're going to videotape each guest with their gift and good wishes with the aid of a video camera and a planned gift-wrapping activity. Rent or borrow a video camera if you haven't one on hand.

Before the shower, ask your guests to bring an unwrapped gift, wrapping paper, and ribbon to the shower. You'll probably have to emphasize the "unwrapped" part of the instructions. Tell everyone you have this little time-saver cooked up for them. That is, they won't have to gift wrap before the shower. Remind them, too, to choose gifts appropriate for mailing. You don't want to be stuck with mailing fragile gifts like a ceramic lamp.

Clean off a large table or several tables because you'll need lots of room for spreading out. Stockpile a generous supply of tape, some extra gift-wrapping paper, scissors, and a large box for mailing, that is strong enough to protect the contents of the box.

Decorate the area with baby shower fixin's and trimmin's and some photos of the new baby with baby's name. Hang the baby's picture with a gorgeous ribbon and bow, or display several photos in a small photo book on the gift table. This may be the only chance for the guests to see the new baby for quite some time.

As the shower gets under way, bring out the video camera and film while each guest describes their gift for baby as they are wrapping it. Encourage them to chat a little about how to use the gift they are displaying for the camera. Should they need a little extra help with the dialog, ask them if there is any family history about the gift or a funny story about raising babies that they could share with the group. At the end of their little presentation, encourage each guest to add a personal message for the new baby and parents.

Don't put the video camera away yet! Record a few minutes of the guests gathered about the refreshment table. The refreshments can be shared with the new parents, too, if you plan the menu with mailing in mind. Cookies and bars are two good mailing possibilities for the special-delivery package. Why not decorate a few cookies or bars with the name and birth date of the baby? They'll add a nice touch to the total package and they'll taste good, too.

At the end of the party, tuck the film into the special delivery package along with the gifts and other goodies. Put address information inside and outside of the package and seal tight.

From start to finish, this shower has spanned the distance between friends and new parents. Your ingenuity will allow everyone to enjoy a very unique shower, and the new parents will receive warm wishes in a package marked "Special Delivery!"

Another Idea: If a video camera isn't available, use a Polaroid camera and take lots of pictures of the party activities and guests. Send the photos with the gift package.

Baby How-To Shower

Today's parents seem to have a wealth of information available about how to bring up baby. However, the trick is to get the new parents and the information together. This is where you come in. Shower the new mother with tips and advice on how to take care of baby, including proven taste-tempting recipes for toddlers.

Send a small package of index cards, with the top card as the invitation asking your guests to give detailed how-to helps for children's activities, holiday decorations, child-preferred recipes, and parenting tips. Your guests will have a chance to show off their knowledge, and the new mother will have the benefit of your guests' combined years of experience. Only you and your guests can give the kind of helpful hints that come with the recommendation "I tried it myself and it works!"

Make sure your request for kinds of how-tos for bringing up baby is clear in your invitation. You'll need to list categories to give your guests some idea about what kinds of helps or tips are appropriate. Your list could include the headings of: Homemade Toys, Rainy Day Activities, Play-Time Learning Techniques, Parenting Tips, Toddler Finger Food Ideas, Clothing for Toddlers, and "Help for Parents" Sources. Add or subtract headings from this list as necessary to fit the needs of the new mother and the interests of the guests.

Each how-to should be written or typed on 3 × 5-inch index cards. Ask your guests to personalize or decorate the cards with drawings, photos, magazine cutouts, or fabric. A little note and name of the giver should be on each card as well as the date. Send at least two cards for each category in case some guests would like to share more than one how-to in the same subject area. After you've sent the cards with the invitations, copy the subject titles at the tops of the index cards. These cards should be in a contrasting color to make them easy to see and to help separate the different categories in the recipe box.

Encourage everyone to bring more helps and hints by letting them know there will be time to copy ideas for their own file (you'll need extra index cards on hand). The more ideas there are to share, the longer the activity will last at your shower. Then, too, you'll find the group discussion at the shower will spark new ideas. Add these to the new mother's collection.

Do yourself and your guests a favor by having plenty of pens on hand. Buy ballpoint pens and tie ½-inch satin ribbon around the top half of each pen. On the ends of the ribbon, in your best script or printing, write "It's a girl!" or "It's a boy!" and add the birth date. Choose pastel-colored pens and white ribbon with gold writing, or pick a color scheme to match your shower colors. The decorated pens make pretty and practical party favors.

Sharing experiences and exchanging ideas that work is what this shower is about. It organizes the "how-to" of child rearing in a fun and supportive setting.

Office Shower

Busy co-workers of the new mom will appreciate this shower idea. You will, too, when you see how you can plan and prepare almost the entire shower at your desk with the help of memos and the telephone.

This shower is going to be planned around lunchtime in the office day. Take a straw vote and decide on the best day – a day when most people will be in the office. Decide, too, on an amount everyone will be willing to spend on the food and gift. Add the guest of honor's lunch to the amount. Then pick up the telephone and order soup and sandwiches or a cracker, fresh fruit, and cheese plate from the local deli.

Still at your desk, pull out your memo pad and direct this invitation to all the department personnel. SUBJECT: A very important target date – This memo takes precedence over all other letters, reports, meetings, etc., etc. Type in the correct information and copy on the copying machine. Or if you like, go back to the Invitations Guide, cut out the printer-ready memo invitation, fill in the necessary information, and photocopy.

A shower isn't a shower without some traditional decorations. So whether your group decides to shower the new mom at her desk or in the company lunchroom, you can still have reminders that this is a baby shower. Since your area is makeshift, think about easy ways to decorate. Baby shower theme napkins are a good choice, as is a party favor basket. Decorate an "In/Out" basket with pink and blue bows and fill with easy-to-make baby shower favors. These simple favors look good and taste good too. Cut out paper baby buggies from colored construction paper (See the Favors, Name Tag and Place Card Guide), and type this jingle on each buggy:

> This chocolate kiss
> Brings our best wish
> For _____ and _____ (insert names of parents)
> New Master or Miss!

Tape a buggy to a foil-wrapped chocolate kiss.

One big group gift usually wins out, so reach for the telephone again and order the gift . . . delivered to the office.

A thoughtful alternative, especially if the gift is large, follows this easy plan. Give instructions to have the gift delivered to the new mom's home on or after the day of the shower. Find a picture of the gift item, either from a brochure or advertisement, and paste it to a light cardboard backing. Draw puzzle-shaped pieces on the back, cut out the pieces, and wrap in a small gift box. When the gift is opened the pieces will have to be put together to solve the gift puzzle.

This gift-wrapping idea saves you the problem of wrestling with wrapping paper and huge boxes and saves the new mom the job of lugging a large gift home from the office. The shower is over, the new mom is pleased with the attention, and you should be very proud of yourself! Even though your desk is piled high with things to do, you didn't let this special occasion go unnoticed. And, best of all, this shower didn't demand a lot of time or a bundle of money.

"It's Twins!" Shower

It doesn't happen all that often, so when twins are born everyone wants to make the baby shower a special occasion. Use this shower to treat the mother and twins with extra attention and compliments. Mom will love the rave notices.

In case the news hasn't spread, send out a unique invitation that can only mean one thing . . . twins! Try something like this:

IT'S TWINS!

Double the babies
Double the fun
We're having a shower
So be sure to come!

If you want to use this verse, you'll find it printer-ready in the Invitations Guide. Cut it out and take it to your local printer. Ask to see their invitation-sized paper.

It would be wonderful if you could have the stars of the shower attend. Fashion a very quiet place for the twins if you must, but do try to have them join the party at some point so everyone can enjoy these double bundles from heaven. If need be, schedule the shower a month after their birth date to be sure they can come to the party.

Plan your decorations to not-so-subtly remind your guests

that we're talking twin power here. Instead of one umbrella at the gift-opening area, use two tied together with a ribbon and bow. Underneath the umbrellas lay two burping cloths with a little note saying "for the best-burped babies." To make, simply add trim to two plain cloth diapers and write the babies' names with a textile marking pen, or embroider. Arange clusters of two balloons each, tied at intervals through the room. Write the twins' names on the balloons. On the guest of honor herself, pin a bow or flower corsage with two pairs of bootees tacked to the center.

Continue to carry out the twin theme at the refreshment table. Place two baby dolls in a small toy doll buggy for the centerpiece. Scatter daisies or carnations around the wheels of the buggy and write the babies' names on the buggy top. Tie a pretty bow with streamers to the buggy handle. For take-home party favors or sugary treats at the party, purchase chocolate "cigars" with the name of each twin. Or bake sugar cookies in the shape of little boys or girls, whatever the case may be. Decorate and write their names with sugar frosting.

Twin-baby shower gifting is easy. When a mother of TWO sets of twins was asked if there were appropriate gifts to give on the occasion of twins she replied succintly, "Two of everything!" Your guests will have a wide range of gifts to choose from, just so long as they choose two of each.

For the twin shower activity, combine a word game with the opening of gifts. This word game is a game of phrases using the words—you guessed it—"two" or "double." Write clues to these phrases ahead of time and quietly slip them under the ribbons of the gift packages as they arrive. As the guest of honor opens a gift, she'll read a clue out loud. The correct answer must be given before the next gift can be opened.

CLUE	ANSWER
two-faced	double-dealing
consisting of two parts	twofold
betrayl	double cross
betting all or nothing	doubling your money
half-price sale	two for the price of one
two slow birds	two turtle doves
multiple difficulty	double trouble
a couple is fun, but more is a throng	two's company, three's a crowd
add this up to get _____	one plus one equals two
more is better	two's better than one
a ballroom dance	the two-step
every transaction is recorded in two parts	double entry

After all the twin puns have been said and each gift has been opened, we can be sure the new mom will leave with a double dose of good choor and best wishes!

Quilting Bee Shower

Take the best of two worlds and use the old-fashioned quilting bee to fashion an up-to-date theme quilt for the new baby. This theme is especially workable for a religious group, card group, or any other group that gets together on a regular basis. You can easily plan the theme for the quilt when the new mother-to-be is absent, work on the individual squares when you have time, and regroup on the day of the shower to finish the quilt among good conversation and refreshments.

For the new little twenty-first-century baby, choose a "When I Grow Up" theme. Each square features a little boy and girl working at an occupation you feel would be quite common in the next century. Remind each other to be careful to avoid any outdated role models. Your group could choose other themes like baby animals, cartoon figures, or symbols of love for the new baby's quilt. Whatever you choose, if you incorporate several colors and a theme that includes girls and boys, you'll be sure to have an appropriate quilt for baby Jane or baby John.

Give yourself at least six weeks before the shower date to agree on a theme and work on the individual quilting squares. At this time you'll decide whether to cross stitch, appliqué or embroider the squares, what type of fabric to work on (is it washable?), and size of squares. It is vital that you pick a firm due date for the squares. Select someone who will be willing to sew the squares together, and name her as the drop-off site for the finished squares. Collect a fee for the backing and batting sections you'll need for finishing the quilt.

On the day of the shower, invite the members to come a little early to help with preparations for the quilting. Baste the batting to the wrong side of the backing. Pin the backing to the top, right sides together, and stitch all around. Leave an opening on one edge and turn the quilt right side out. When the new mother-to-be comes, the quilt will be ready for tying and finishing.

Getting into the spirit of things as you work on the "When I Grow Up" quilt, try to imagine, out loud, what the future will hold for these little ones. Agree to write down your predictions in a small booklet and present it along with the quilt to the new mother. It's a little like a time capsule for the new baby to read when he or she is well into the twenty-first century.

This shower is a combination of cooperative effort, good conversation, and an old-time feeling of warm regard for each other. And as the last thread end is snipped, could we stretch our inmaginations and see this baby's quilt as a magic carpet carrying baby safely into the future?

Another Idea: The new mother is sure to love the quilt, but in case someone else has already thought of the idea, why not try other projects? Consider quilting bumper pads for the crib, a wall-hanging for the nursery, or a colorful pad for the playpen. Or, try this quick project. Stitch together a patchwork of terry cloth washcloths for baby's diaper-changing pad. Arrange white cloths for every other square. At the shower, give your guests textile marking pens in bright, primary colors and let them draw or write on the white squares. The combined creativity will result in an uniquely personal gift.

Solve the Mystery Shower

Shades of Sherlock Holmes! This shower activity turns your friends into super-sleuths, ready and able to solve a jewelry heist mystery. Invitations and gift-opening time will be written into the script designed especially for fun baby shower entertainment.

You can be the sole mastermind of this shower activity, but the mystery writing is easier and certainly more fun with two heads working together. It's easy if you plot your mystery in steps.

Now put your thinking cap on, because you're going to write a script that involves the theft of jewelry inherited by the new heir of a famous family. At the shower your guests will act out the roles of the characters you create for your story and then spend time solving the mystery together. Remember, your script doesn't have to be professional.

First, decide when and where the action is to take place, then create a reason for the characters to be together. For example, a 1930s Hollywood movie mogul and his starlet wife have invited friends to their home on the occasion of presenting their new heir. Flesh out the story with a sequence of events leading up to the jewelry theft. At the same time, set up a list of characters, all with a background and history that seem to show a motive for stealing the jewels.

Assign a character to each guest and, using the name of this character, send an invitation to this fictional event. Underneath add, "You are really cordially invited to the home

of _____ for a baby shower." Be sure to add the real
time, date, and address.

Include a guest list with the invitation and a small descrip-
tion of each fictional guest. Your list might look like this:
"Luella Parsnips, a nosy gossip columnist who is being
threatened by a gangster because of her gambling debts":or
"Miss Meow, the new baby's nurse, who took the job to get
out of the cat burglar profession." Give a brief outline of each
character's background so everyone can "get into character"
before the shower.

At the bottom of the invitation let your guests know if
costumes are required. You'll have to decide how many real
"hams" are coming to the shower and if they would enjoy
dressing up.

In the same envelope or in a second mailing, send clues that
point to the thief or reveal secrets about other characters, es-
tablishing possible motives or opportunities for stealing the
jewels. Ask some of the guests to enclose the clues sent to
them in the shower gift. This is a good way to include gift-
opening time into the mystery itself. As the gifts are
opened – planned for a time after the heist and after you have
started to solve the mystery, the guest of honor will read the
clues out loud.

When each guest arrives on the day of the shower, give a
list of sequenced, timed directions planned especially for
their character. This will help you to move people about,
plant red herrings, and give the thief the opportunity to steal
the jewels.

To bring some direction to the mystery solving, appoint
someone as detective, who will take charge of the discussion.
To help the detective with the job, draw up a list of appropriate questions to bring the group to the solution of the crime.
Although the detective acts as a moderator, he or she should
have no advance knowledge of the jewel thief's identity.

You'll be wise to set an agreed-upon time for the mystery
to be solved so that the shower doesn't last too long. Save

time for refreshments, during which everyone can rehash the mystery.

A good mystery involves plenty of red herrings pointing the finger of suspicion at each of the characters. But when all is said and done, only one character should clearly have the means, opportunity, and motive for stealing the jewels. This is a fun shower for everyone and an especially good activity for a couples shower. Once the detecting is over and the crime is solved, you can be sure that everyone will have had an arresting good time!

Next-To-New Shower

You know that your shower guests are all going to be millionaires someday, but today isn't that day! When prospects are somewhat limited, host a shower asking only for used baby presents! That's right, only baby items from garage sales and thrift stores or hand-me-down family stuff are acceptable. Who knows – someone may come across a first-rate antique for the new little Josephine or Napoleon Bonaparte.

Since classified ads play a major role in finding next-to-new items, word your invitation in the form of a want ad. Type the invitation in a newspaper column style like this:

GUESTS WANTED
with party experience for
Cindy's baby shower. Need
expert celebrators June 8,
6-8 P.M. for shared potluck
supper at Mary Smith's house.
Bring gifts that are hand-me-
down family stuff or next-to-
new items only!

Some gift ideas to tell your guests to keep an eye out for are a secondhand car seat, crib, bassinet, cradle, bathtub, toy chest, high chair, baby blankets and clothing, toys, and books. Don't overlook favorite child-care books.

If your guests do come upon a great furniture find, check to see that the paint finish is lead-free. If in doubt, they should remove the old paint job and re-do with lead-free paint. Furniture made after 1978 is required to have a lead-free paint finish. Of course any baby gift should be checked to see that it is accident-safe.

When you're at the thrift store or garage sale look for a well-worn baby shoe that can be used for the baby-shoe-melt guessing game at the shower. Dip the shoe in a water-filled container (something like a cut-off quart-sized milk carton works best) and freeze. Strip off the cardboard, set the ice block in a dish on the gift table,and ask the guests to guess how long it will take the ice to melt. The person guessing closest to the time wins the prize. The prize? What else but a novelty ice cube tray!

Rustle up a quick gift idea to serve as a decorative carrier for the shower gifts as well as a bassinet for baby. Find a used oval clothes basket and pad the basket with a foam pillow covered with waterproof material. Slip a pillowcase around the foam pillow as a sheet for the pad. Finish off the basket by attaching bows, using the same color scheme as the pillowcase, around the rim. Set the bassinet on the gift table as a collecting spot for the other shower gifts.

To simplify refreshments, plan a potluck supper so there will be little in the way of effort or expense for you as the hostess. Ask each guest to bring a food contribution for this informal meal. Set the supper table, put on the coffee, and your preparations will be complete.

If you would like to fuss a little, make some party-pretty paper ice cream cones for the centerpiece. Take brown wrapping paper, cut into 5-inch squares and roll up diagonally from corner to corner to make the cone. Then top off the cones with ice cream (yellow and pink cosmetic balls). Arrange the cones haphazardly around a grouping of small stuffed animals found at the thrift store.

When everyone is on a tight budget, this practical and inexpensive shower can be counted on to provide an "easy street" of fun and celebration time.

First-Time Grandmother's Shower

This shower is a fun and friendly get-together that recognizes the joy of the first-time grandmother. Invite friends and neighbors who will be happy to share in the excitement of the new baby's arrival. Bake a super-rich dessert, put on the coffee, and get ready to enjoy an old-fashioned coffee klatch.

When you have this shower could be as important as deciding to have the shower in the first place. After all, if you have the shower after the baby has arrived, grandmother will have the opportunity to show off her pictures. So set your shower date for a time when you know the new grandmother will have plenty of pictures to share.

Gift giving may seem unnecessary, but when you think about it, grandmother may need to be showered with baby necessities too. A few extra baby things always come in handy when baby visits.

Gifts such as extra diapers, baby bottles, blankets, or a high chair and portable crib that everyone chips in to buy are going to make baby's visits easier for grandmother. Then again, you can keep the gift-giving simple with a baby's care caddy. Decorate a box or basket and ask guests to fill with baby powder, lotion, soap, shampoo, diapers, diaper pins, and a pacifier. Tuck in some fun gifts, too, like a grandmother's bragging photo book or a bumper sticker that carries the message "Foxy Grandmother!"

If this foxy new grandmother hasn't told the whole world yet about this happy event, you can help her out. Tack up a large banner outside the front door or garage. The message should read loud and clear that your guest of honor is a first-time grandmother. Print in large letters a message like this: "SHELLY MADE GRANDMOTHER STATUS! TUES-DAY, MAY 26."

Just so there is no mistaking that this get-together is a shower, serve a pretty shower umbrella cake. Mix your favorite round layer-cake recipe or prepare the ready-mix kind and bake in two round layer pans. After the cakes have cooled and are out of the pans, score and cut them into the shape of umbrellas. Frost the cakes and decorate with tiny sugar flowers. Use a contrasting line of icing for the "ribs" of the umbrella. You'll find the instructions and illustrations showing how to cut the cake into an umbrella shape in the Recipe Guide.

While you serve the umbrella cake with coffee, you can tease the now grandmother that this dessert may be one of her last. She can't possibly serve these sinfully sweet desserts to her grandchild, or the tooth fairy will get her!

This shower is clearly designed to allow the new grandmother to share her happiness in this landmark occasion with her friends and neighbors. It's not your ordinary shower, but then becoming a grandmother for the first time isn't an ordinary event!

Bag a Lunch

Are your friends, including the new mom, in the superwoman category? And the only time you see them together is at the exercise class? Then think about bringing the shower to them with this theme idea. Grab some decorations, bag some treats in decorated bags, and your surprise shower will be ready.

Since you are a member of this super-woman group, too, you probably won't have time to send invitations. Just quietly pass the word around at one of your classes. Of course, let your instructor in on the plans so you won't be surprised with a last-minute change of date for that particular class.

Ahead of time buy some banners, balloons, and paper streamers at your local party store. These will be easy to carry to class and you'll use them to decorate the gift-opening area. Don't forget to bring plenty of tape and string for the balloons. Cunning little you will have already thought ahead about how your friends can help blow up the balloons and tape the banners and streamers in place.

The only real time you're going to spend on this shower is when decorating the bags and preparing the lunch. To carry out the baby shower theme, take a white lunch bag and trim it with sheeplike ears and "wool" and write the announcement of "NEW BA-A-ABY!" on the front. Here's how: Find white lunch bags at a party-supply store, or ask if you can buy a few white bags from your local bakery. Using white construction paper, cut out two ovals about 2½ inches long, and fold lengthwise for the ears. With the top edge of the bag folded over, draw black eyes and mouth on the folded section of the bag. On the bottom section of the bag, print in large letters "NEW BA-A-ABY!" Place a light lunch in the bag, and tape the ears between the bag and foldover top on either side. For the sheep's wool, paste cotton or acrylic cosmetic balls on the top edge of the foldover section.

Plan your lunch menu with the same time-saving consideration. Since it's an exercise class, you'll probably want to lean toward the healthy kind of food like whole-grain bread and fresh vegetables rather then gooey cupcakes. A simple bag lunch menu like a sandwich, salad or fresh vegetables and a peanut butter cookie for dessert will be appreciated. Whatever you decide on, remember, these bags may be standing at room temperature for some time, so stay away from mayonnaise and other foods that need to be kept very hot or cold to be safe to eat.

After class is over and it's time to begin the party, yell "surprise!" and blindfold your guest of honor. This is the time when you can hand out the streamers and balloons and have everyone help decorate the guest of honor's chair and gift-giving area. Place the gifts around the chair and have the new mother sit down. Remove the blindfold and enjoy the look of surprise on her face.

Opening the gifts and sharing a light lunch together should only take an hour or so. But in this short period of time, the new mother will have lovely gifts and the pleasure of receiving good wishes from her friends.

This shower idea is very adaptable to any class, club meeting, or office situation where your friends are gathered together. You'll need only an hour or so of time squeezed in before, during, or after. Wherever the meeting place, this shower theme will prove to be extremely portable and flexible. This is one shower that's easily "in the bag"!

Another Idea: Gather the tops of pastel-colored lunch bags together, tie tightly with a pretty ribbon, and add a baby rattle, diaper pins, or talcum bottle to the bow. After lunch, the baby items can be given to the new mother as extra gifts.

Baby Stitchery Shower

Some new mothers believe baby's layette isn't complete without embroidered or cross-stitched bibs and blankets. Aren't you glad you know someone like this? This will give you just the excuse you need for a traditional and personalized needlework theme.

Stitch up a complete baby gift during the shower. Whether you make it a group effort or an individual project, you and your guests will have to do a bit of gift pre-planning to ensure a successful stitchery shower. The main thing to keep in mind is to find projects that can be finished in 1 or 2 hours. That way you'll be able to give finished gifts to the new mother at the end of the shower. Don't forget to find a project for the new mother to work on as well, so that she'll feel a part of the group effort.

If your guests are having trouble coming up with good ideas, give them this list of small project suggestions:

prefinished bibs and bonnets, sachet bag kits, needleworked birth records, crafty crib mobiles, "SHHH!" door signs, and tooth-pocket pillows. Some especially good ideas come from Designing Women Unltd.(you'll find them in the Address Guide). Their thermal fabric receiving blankets and baby shirts are prefinished and only need a simple cross-stitched pattern to finish them off. Susan Burge, co-owner of Designing Women, Unltd., says the stitch count for the thermal fabric is approximately five stitches to the inch, so a project goes really fast. Cross-stitch designs can be ordered from them as well. A crib blanket with a design worked in the center section area is also available. Several people at the shower could work on it at the same time.

You should be able to find all of these items at craft or needlework shops. If your local shop doesn't carry these items, write to the companies listed in the Address Guide for the best way to obtain these kits.

Save your list of resources. It will serve as a party favor to give your guests at the shower. Anyone who enjoys needlework projects likes to add to her collection of patterns and resources. Also the new mother may need an address to help add to her baby's wardrobe.

Since the main activity of this shower depends on your guests working on a project, you'll need comfortable chairs and plenty of light. It wouldn't hurt to have some kind of flat surface space available for everyone too. You'll probably find yourself setting up chairs around the dining room table, or using TV trays or end tables. Even though you assume each guest will bring their own scissors and needles, it still would be wise for you to have extra sewing supplies on hand.

Well, before we know it, the time is up and everyone is admiring the finished projects. After the needlework show is over and the new mother has been presented with her gifts, bring out the surprise gift from the group . . . a pretty fabric diaper bag either purchased or made beforehand by some of the members of the group. This diaper bag is going to be the gift box and wrapping paper for all the shower gifts.

As our new mom leaves with her bag of beautiful needleworked gifts, you can be sure these gifts and the good
time spent at this shower will be long remembered.

Queen for a Day

What could be more appropriate then treating the new
mom like a queen for the day? Take advantage of this theme
and dramatize it to the fullest extent. Present a program of
speakers (friends and relatives of the guest of honor)
reminiscing about moments in her life.

Send the queen a fresh flower or silk corsage first thing in
the morning to begin her royal day. At the appointed time,
arrange to have a private car, taxi, limousine, or horse-
drawn carriage available for her leisurely journey to the
shower. Roll out the red carpet (a long roll of paper will do)
from her vehicle to the door. The guests should already be
there, seated around small tables. As she enters, everyone
stands and gives her a warm round of applause. Escort the
queen to her royal chair, prominently centered in front of her
audience. You can turn any available chair into a chair fit for
royalty with a fake fur or a royal purple fabric throw cover.

With a roll of drums or spoons clinking on the edge of glasses proclaim from a scroll the new mother as "queen of the en-
chanted land of new babies." Set a gold paper crown on her
head (see directions in the Decoration Guide), and present
the scroll to her . . . all of this done with dramatic flourish-
es and bowing.

As emcee, begin the program of guest speakers you have
prearranged. Find friends and relatives who can tell a good
story, and ask them to recall some childhood scrapes or em-
barrassing moments to contribute to this review of the
queen's "royal life." Encourage each speaker to share mostly
laugh-provoking experiences, but allow some tender and
serious moments to slip into the program, too. Every so often, between speakers, present the queen with a few shower

gifts which then can be passed around to the guests. End the program by bringing the queen to the table area where the guests are already seated. It would be appropriate here to propose a toast to the queen with a small glass of fruit juice. Serve a simple main dish, salad, roll, and dessert. Joyce St. Angelo of Minnetonka, Minnesota, used the Flowerpot Dessert as a decorative addition to her shower. Fill small, red clay pots with ice cream, top with crushed sandwich cookie "dirt" and a fresh or silk flower. The flower can later be given as a take-home favor. Set the frozen flowerpots on the tables at the beginning of the shower as an attractive centerpiece, and they'll be thawed just enough for some scrumptious dessert eating. See complete directions in the Recipe Guide.

This shower lends itself to several different locations. Whether you decide on your home, religious center, or community room, you'll add to the happy memories of the new mother.

Family-Style Shower

Since relatives have a way of getting excited over news of an addition to the family, some of you may want to hold a family-style shower to welcome the new member. Yes, even dads, brothers, and grandpas are invited to this shower. The point is to have everyone from both sides of the family welcome the new baby.

Help get the conversation rolling between the two families with a garden picture gallery. With a little quiet sleuthing on your part, you should be able to dig up baby pictures from each side of the family. Don't forget to ask for the new baby's picture, too, to complete the picture gallery.

Once you have the pictures in hand, you can start framing the pictures for the garden gallery. Cut out tulips, daisies, and bachelor's buttons from brightly colored construction paper or posterboard. Add green stems and leaves made from the same material. The size of the flower frame will depend on the size of your pictures. The picture should fit nicely in the center of the flower. Tape one baby picture to each flower head and write the name underneath. Now turn an empty wall into a garden gallery by taping the flowers at a convenient height for viewing.

On the day of the shower, the picture gallery garden will be just the icebreaker you need to get everyone comfortable. While your guests enjoy a refreshment they can wander over to the garden picture gallery. They won't need any conversation starter from you because they'll have plenty of comments to make about the baby pictures. As the conversation gets livelier you'll hear, "Baby has his mother's eyes!" or "That chin definitely runs in the Smith family!"

Once everyone is comfortable with each other, start the main activity of the shower . . . baby's memory book. This memory book is going to be a little different. Why? Because the focus is on the relatives instead of the baby. This book will reveal fun and interesting things about the baby's relatives. It's going to record their favorite things, activities they were engaged in when baby was born, and any world or community events they thought were important or newsworthy.

Fashion a memory book made of 8½ x 5½-inch sheets with two holes punched at the top. Type or write "fill in the blank" sentences on the sheets beforehand. A sample of the form used for Baby's Memory Book follows. To give a more professional look to the memory book take the form to your local fast printer and have the material printed on 8½ x 5½-inch sheets.

Hand out one sheet per guest and ask each one to complete the sentences.

WELCOME BABY _____(name)

FROM _____(your name)

I suppose you could describe me as _____

_____

My favorite things are _____

places are _____

friends are _____

hobbies are _____

work is _____

I consider the most newsworthy event that occurred
when you were born to be _____

_____

On the day you were born I _____

_____

After everyone has finished, collect the sheets and tie a
narrow ribbon through the holes. Present to the parents of
the new baby.

Your guests are going to be curious and wonder what
everybody else considered a newsworthy event. So it would
be fun to let everyone have time to share their newsworthy
happening before going on to the opening of gifts. If someone
from the group doesn't ask, wonder out loud what event was
mentioned the most times as being a newsworthy event.

Gift-giving time can be another occasion to highlight the
special bringing together of two families by presenting the
new parents with a framed family tree. It will show the
merging of two families with the newest little addition at the
center. An artist or calligrapher can make a beautiful family
tree design from the information you've collected beforehand.

During this shower the members of both families have an
opportunity to get to know each other a little bit better, and

a warm welcome is extended to the newest branch of the family tree!

Another Idea: The activities in this shower theme can be easily adapted for baby's christening party.

ShowerWise Gift Themes

T his section is for you when imagination seems to fail you. If you're concerned about giving the same kind of shower over and over, turn your attention to gifting as a way of adding a little extra something to your shower. Once you decide on a gift theme, ideas for invitations, activities, and decorations will fall into place. Look through this offering of gift themes to find an easy way to add sparkle to your shower.

Baby Registry Shower

Solve the gift-giving dilemma with a preference list from the baby registry, or "stork club" as it is commonly called, of your favorite department or children's store. Urge the new mother to sign up at a baby registry. Your guests will save time and, better yet, there'll be no gift duplications. This is how the baby registry works. The new mother fills out a preference list of gifts at her favorite store or department. This list is available to anyone who would like to purchase a gift for the new mother. You'll find the preferred clothing, nursery items, feeding supplies, traveling equipment, and furniture to choose from. As purchases are made, the list is updated to reflect items that are still available.

At the shower you can make this theme a bit more interesting and fun by playing gift charades. As in regular charades, in which each syllable of a word is represented by a dramatic action, the guest of honor will act out each syllable of the gift that she has just opened. If she wishes, she may choose someone in the group to act out the word. As each gift is guessed, the guest of honor goes on to open the next gift.

One way to make sure everyone puts their heart and soul into this game is to award the winners with refreshments served by the losing group. Give prizes to the winning group as well. With stakes like these it won't be too hard to whip up lots of enthusiasm. Divide the guests into two groups, and may the best team enjoy their service!

"Bear" Necessities Shower

Gift the new mother with essentials like T-shirts, sweaters, sunsuits, crib toys, blankets, sleeper sets, or a walker . . . all decorated with bears! As for any theme-related gift giving, you'll want to make sure that all your guests are aware of the shower theme before they go shopping. They'll get the message if you word your invitations something like this: "Bear a gift . . . anything that reminds you of a cuddly bear!" See the printer-ready invitation in the Invitations Guide.

Decorate your shower area with the same kinds of bear details. Set plush bears with armfuls of balloons on tables, bookshelves, and mantels. Sprinkle illustrated The Three

Bears and Winnie The Pooh storybooks around the room. Make a special effort to find bear designs on paper plates, cups, and napkins for the refreshment table. Some card and party shops have nice designs. Skip the flowers and bake a bear centerpiece for the refreshment table. You can create an almost-too-loveable-to-eat teddy bear from your favorite bread dough. See Recipe Guide for shaping and baking instructions. Set the teddy bear (or bears) in a breadbasket and tie a color-coordinated bow around the bear's neck.

Private Moments Shower

Turn the gift tables around and concentrate on the new mother rather than on baby for gift ideas. The new mother may be at just the stage of pregnancy where she is going to need and appreciate mood lighteners. Little gifts to pamper her while she's in the hospital should bring a smile and sincere thanks.

Hand-care products like a favorite nail polish, emery boards, nail polish remover, and a fragrant hand lotion are gifts that will make her feel like her old self again. Give books and magazines for her reading pleasure, and add a feminine bed jacket and slippers for that looking-pretty feeling.

Just for fun, after the gift giving, ask your guests to jot down their best guess about the time of the new baby's arrival, weight, and sex. Have each guest sign their name, make a small wager, and seal their bets in small envelopes. It'll be your job as hostess to open the envelopes after the stork has come and send the winnings to the person who has the most right answers.

Cookie Bake Shower

The household schedule seems to change drastically once baby arrives, especially mealtimes. Said one mother about the new baby experience: "Expectations of home-cooked desserts every night quickly change to the realities of a serving of ice cream for dessert." After this shower, at least there will be a home-baked cookie with the ice cream.

As for the sewing bee, everyone brings their handiwork to the shower. In this case the handiwork is a batch of favorite cookie dough ready to drop onto cookie sheets. Each guest takes a turn baking their cookie dough in the oven.

While the cookies are baking, there will be time for making good conversation, exchanging recipes, and snacking on freshly baked cookies.

Since this shower is so informal, arrange gift giving at the kitchen table during the baking time. Traditional gifts are always acceptable, but include cookie cutters spelling out baby's name, a cake pan shaped as baby's initial, or a musical revolving birthday cake tray to highlight the theme of this shower.

This shower holds off the dessert hungries with freezer bags of unique and yummy shower gifts.

Another Idea: Prepare casseroles as a group project. Everyone brings two or three basic ingredients. At the shower, assign each person to a work station and get them started on chopping, sautéing, and precooking. Give the guest of honor the finished dishes in plastic freezer bags and foil baking pans.

"IOU" Shower

For gifts that money can't buy, hold an IOU shower. Each gift, written on IOU blanks, is a promise of help or service to the new parents. IOU gifts stand out from purchased gifts because the guests are giving of themselves.

Each IOU can be planned to give the parents extra time, a little pampering, or needed information. Any new parent will enjoy a Saturday morning housecleaning, a homemade pie, a home permanent, directions for how to play "Itsy, Bitsy Spider", a grocery shopping trip, a complete chili supper, or free hours of babysitting! An older friend and experienced mother volunteered a free midnight consultation on baby care in anticipation of that night when nothing seems to work.

Make up blank IOU's on index cards to look like this:

IOU: _____

FROM: _____

AVAILABLE:_____

PHONE: _____

Send three or four cards in each invitation, and ask the guests to fill out as many as they wish. Remind your guests that the IOU's should be wrapped as a baby shower gift.

On the day of the shower, have on hand a box to hold the index cards, extra index cards, and subject file separators. Organize the file box with headings on the file separators, such as household tasks, baby care, and food. The new parents will eventually use up the extra index cards with their own list of names and services needed throughout the year.

This box of IOU's will be a loving reminder that "Help given in time of need is a gift indeed!"

Disposable Shower

It's a disposable and convenient world out there, so let's give the new parents all the handy, use-and-throw products available. If it's for baby and it's disposable, wrap it up and bring it along.

Suggest such disposable gift items as baby swabs, facial tissues, baby wipes, and diapers, diapers, diapers! Wrap all gifts in white tissue paper with big red letters that say "DISPOSABLE." Add one large wastebasket decorated with ribbons and bows to do double duty – collecting used wrapping paper and carrying gifts home.

Let's not forget the party appointments. You can easily find fashionable paper plates, cups, napkins, coasters, streamers, and decorations that will fit in with your disposables theme. Paper hats, paper party whistles, and paper chains will all add to the charm.

Since there will be lots of diapers around, there should definitely be an old-fashioned diaper-changing lesson and contest, especially if this is a mixed-couples shower. Announce loudly to the group that any tips or words of advice will be welcome at this lesson and contest. When you feel the new parents have endured enough smart remarks during this session, toast them with a sincere and heartfelt "Bottoms up!"

ShowerWise
Sprinkles

J ust as I was ready to turn off my word processor for what I thought was a well-deserved break, I saw ShowerWise do a little soft-shoe again. "Hold onto your umbrella!" warned ShowerWise. "There are still imaginative bits of ideas and special touches for showers that we haven't covered yet."

Intrigued, I posed my fingers over the keyboard and waited.

"You see," ShowerWise continued, "with bits or germs of an idea, anyone can go on to create a shower perfectly suited to them."

"Yes," I said, "just as every shower starts with a sprinkle . . ."

" . . . every party begins with an idea!" a self-satisfied ShowerWise finished for me. And so, here is a sprinkling of ideas to get you started toward planning a memorable and fun baby shower.

Puzzle Olympics Shower

No need to puzzle out this shower. Plan a puzzle contest using 500-piece puzzles. Look for babies, toys, dolls, and so on as puzzle subjects. Spread out the puzzle pieces on each table, allow guests to draw numbers for tables, and set the timer for 30 minutes. The table that finishes first or comes closest to finishing their puzzle wins a prize.

Saving Delight Shower

Shower your thrifty-minded friend with cents-off coupons for baby supplies. Enclose a coupon folder with each invitation for easy coupon gathering. Continue the coupon clipping as a group activity during the shower and top off this savings orgy with a subscription to a coupon saving newsletter.

Victorian-Style Shower

Lace and ribbon play a key role in this shower. Send off perfect-penmanship invitations on white or cream stationery with lace trim pasted on the edges. Wrap large white ribbon bows around the backs of chairs, and dress the table with a lace tablecloth or runner. Complete the Victorian setting with servings of petit fours on paper doilie liners. Coffee and tea are served in your collection of bone china cups and saucers.

Mission Possible Shower

Do you want to have a shower at an out-of-the-way location but you're afraid it will be too much of a hassle for the guests? Turn this obstacle into a plus by making the location part of the shower theme. Give the shower invitation a spy-mission flavor with this cryptic instruction at the end: "Your mission is to find the secret meeting at the appointed time, and ENJOY!" Draw a detailed map showing how to get to the location – whether park, beach area, or secluded cabin – and enclose it with the invitation in an envelope marked "Secret!"

Collection Mania Shower

Turn the current craze for collecting to your advantage and plan your shower theme around a special collection for baby. Whatever the choice – stamps, dolls, trains, coins, or thimbles – baby and parents will cherish this collection for years to come.

Color Consultant Shower

If the new mother is anxious to get back to "normal-size" clothes and into fashion again, she'll enjoy the help of a color consultant. Get the whole group into the act, finding and sampling colors that will have them looking their best. Treat all your guests to their personal color palette as a take-home party favor.

Setting-A-Record Shower

No, you're not going to plan the longest shower ever given . . . you are going to shower the new mom with record-keeping supplies. A baby's album, medical records book, growth chart, and babysitting emergency information will give a good start towards recording baby's accomplishments and necessities. If this baby sets any records, mom will be well prepared!

Designer Diaper Shower

This shower stretches the gift-opening activity time even though the group has decided to chip in for one large gift. Ask each guest to bring a small gift as well (cotton swabs, petroleum jelly, rattles, baby socks. rubber pants, etc.), all wrapped in a designer diaper! The choice of style or material is limited only by one's imagination. Anything goes . . . decorated disposable diapers, flannel, lace, toweling, silk . . . just so it resembles a diaper. Let the word out that prizes will be awarded for the best-designed, funniest, and most clever diaper.

Treasure Chest Shower

Make or buy a toy chest and decorate it to look like a treasure chest. Ask your guests to bring storage-intended treasures for the chest, such as clothes hangers, pant or skirt hangers, laundry bag, shelf-lining paper, and diaper pail. Serve a picnic-style lunch individually packed in bandana squares.

Picture-Perfect Shower

It's a known fact! Having a new baby brings out the shutterbug in all of us. Picture the perfect gift for the new parents–camera, film, albums, light meter, or video equipment–everything to help baby's step-by-step progress. Frame your invitations with adhesive photo corners stuck kitty-corner onto slightly larger sheets of paper.

Heirloom Shower

Here's a chance for great, great-aunt Bertha to pass on a cherished family heirloom to the new generation. If family heirlooms are in short supply, give found antiques. Old books, an old music box, and a silver brush and comb set are just a few objects that would be appreciated. The mood to strive for here is the charm and wisdom of yesteryear.

Handwriting Analysis Shower

Give everyone a gift at this shower, with an analysis of their handwriting. Ask the analyst (find one in the Yellow Pages under "Handwriting Analysts") to focus on those characteristics that point toward successful parenting. Guests may want to ask questions in a different area that is of more interest to them. After all is said and done, you'll receive a positive analysis of this shower idea.

Pre-Game Shower

Sports fans will go for this shower idea. Open up the trunk, get out those lounge chairs, and enjoy pre-game shower fun and food. Give gifts related to the game, such as a ball with baby's name and shower date and autographed by the players of the favorite team.

Baby Trivia Shower

Skip an evening of playing trivia games? Never! Not when playing trivia will lend itself so well as an activity for your shower. Base this game loosely on today's popular trivia games with questions galore about babies . . . famous babies, baby care, or personal questions about the guest of honor's baby years. The sillier or more outlandish the questions are, the more fun it will be. This shower is designed exclusively for trivial addicts – and anyone who enjoys a good time.

Fairy Godmother Shower

Reenact the childhood story of the fairy godmothers gathered 'round the little princess's cradle. Instead of having them wave their wands, ask each potential fairy godmother to fill out a certificate good for sharing one personal skill with the child in the future. Anything goes, from fly-fishing to math tutoring. Set a whimsical theme for this shower with a pinch of fairy dust (glitter) added to the invitation envelope.

Chinese New Year Shower

If your shower date lands at the end of January or the beginning of February, consult the Chinese zodiac to find out which animal sign will symbolize baby's birth year. This sign and its characteristics can then be given in the shower invitation. Now that you have their attention, ensure attendance at your shower with a promise that each guest will learn his or her personal animal sign and characteristics. Decorate the shower area with the twelve animal signs of the Chinese zodiac, set off sparklers to welcome the new year, and present fortune cookies for dessert.

Valentine Shower

Transform the shower area into a Cupid's retreat with red and white streamers, large and small bows, and red hearts everywhere. Send off invitations on homemade valentine notes asking this question: "What part of Valentine's Day is the same spelled backwards or forwards?" The answer is "noon"! For a wing-flapping finale, serve a heart-shaped pastry with a red berry topping.

Mardi Gras Shower

Seize the opportunity before Lent to shower the new mom with a Mardi Gras. Fashion masks – either-hand held or the kind secured around the head with a rubber band – are de rigueur. Decorate the gift and refreshment table with crepe paper and paper roses to resemble Mardi Gras parade floats. Scatter confetti and chocolate coins wrapped in gold paper everywhere and play celebration music to bring out the Mardi Gras spirit in everyone.

Luck-Of-The-Irish Shower

Once your leprechaun has sent off the paper four-leaf clover invitations, turn your attention to the gift-opening area. Color a cardboard rainbow and prop it on a table against the wall. Wrap a large pot in gold foil and set it in front of the rainbow area. As your guests arrive, stack the gifts casually in and around the pot. Chocolate-mint brownies and Irish coffee will convince everyone that they've found their pot of gold!

"Hello Spring" Shower

What better way to say hello to the new baby than to celebrate the season of new beginnings! Invite your guests to a "get-up-with-the-birds" breakfast. Send invitations with drawings of baby birds peeping in their nest. Carry out the spring theme on the refreshment table with an artificial bird's-nest centerpiece and a bouquet of daffodils.

May Day Shower

Serve a fresh fruit salad with a sprinkling of coconut in wishing wells (see Recipe Guide). Prop a tiny paper umbrella in each well. Twist colorful streamers from a ribbon-wrapped cardboard maypole (cardboard wrapping-paper tube) to tiny baskets of flowers at each place setting. These flower baskets can serve as pretty take-home May basket treats for your guests.

Midsummer Night Shower

Light up a warm summer's night with candles—scented candles, floating candles, and tapered candles in potted plants. Serve a candlelit buffet with harp music playing softly in the background. You'll start a family tradition if you give a decoupage candle with baby's picture and birth information, to be used at subsequent birthday parties.

"Shades of Campfire Days" Shower

Watch the sun go down in your favorite park or beach setting. Set up lanterns and serve a campfire-style spread with s'mores for dessert. Anyone for a really good scary ghost story?

Harvest Moon Shower

Select fall colors for the decorating scheme, set an arrangement of spider mums on the refreshment table, and feature a large cornucopia filled to overflowing with baby gifts. Start refreshments with hot apple cider in mugs followed by a cheese fondue with crunchy French bread. Top it all off with a serving of pumpkin pie.

The Littlest Angel Shower

How do you make your baby shower a standout at holiday time? Create a heavenly shower with angels – paper angel invitations, angel tree ornaments, and angel food cake with coffee. Paste cutout cherub wings to the baby's picture to introduce the newest littlest angel.

ShowerWise Steps

H old on now," I interrupted, "I don't mean to put you in a stall in the middle of your flight, but it seems to me that some of our readers are going to need a simple, basic list to help them plan their shower."

"Of course!" ShowerWise quickly agreed. "I'll be happy to take them by the wing tip . . . Ah, I mean the hand and walk them, step-by-step, through all the how-tos of planning and putting on a party-perfect shower."

Well, ShowerWise was true to her word. She not only gave twelve steps to a successful shower, but she added a shower-planning sheet as well. And for those of you interested in learning about all the right moves a hostess should make at the shower, take a look at the Shower Protocol section.

Twelve Steps to a Successful Shower

How would you like to reduce pre-party panic feelings to just a few minor jitters? It is possible if you have a good plan and can get yourself organized in all major areas. The key is organization. The best way we know of to take the pressure off is the checklist system. Make a complete checklist for every detail. If necessary, make a list for each day, and especially for the day and hours just before you shower. When you know you're accomplishing necessary things every day, your enthusiasm will remain high. You won't think . . . not even for a minute . . . "Why did I get myself into this?"

With a well-thought-out plan, you'll have ample time to arrange for extra help and to borrow or rent whatever you need. You may even be able to "take five" before your guests arrive because you've already checked on the ice cubes and coped with last-minute emergencies. Then, if anyone offers to help, you'll be so organized you can assign things they'll enjoy . . . and you can relax and enjoy your own party.

Use these steps, along with our Shower Planning Sheet, themes, and guides to help you plan your party easily and successfully.

1) Guests: Consult with the new mother or new parents to ensure a complete guest list.

2) Time: Select the day and hour of your shower while you're clearing the guest list. Make sure most guests can attend.

3) Browse through our ShowerWise Themes and Shower-Wise Sprinkles for a plan you think everyone will enjoy.

4) Location: Pick a location that will accommodate the number of potential guests and that will work in with your theme (private home, VFW hall, park. See our Unusual Locations Guide).

5) Invitations: Invitations may be purchased or hand-made(see our Invitations Guide for ideas). Mail them to arrive at least four weeks before your shower date. Include this information, as well as further directions or instructions:

- For (name of persons being honored)
- Date (before or after the baby's arrival)
- Time (most convenient time for everyone)
- Place (location of shower–home, restuarant, club, etc.)
- Kind (general, theme, personal, etc.)
- Baby Registry At (store name and location)
- Given By (hostess and host, co-hostess, etc.)
- R.S.V.P. (name and phone number of person to call for acceptance or "Regrets")

6) Food: Decide who will prepare the food–you, a caterer, restaurant, your guests, or someone else. If you engage someone else to do it, have a clear understanding of exactly what will be provided and the cost. If you will be doing it, plan every detail. Make a shopping list from your recipes and do as much as you can ahead of time. Be sure your kitchen facilities can handle everything you've planned to prepare at your shower (enough oven space and surface burners, ample room in the refrigerator). Plan your silverware, plates, salad bowls, dessert dishes, glasses, cups and saucers, serving dishes, ash trays, candle holders, and so on. (See our Table Setup Guide for tips on how to set up a buffet, a sit-down luncheon or supper, and a dessert-only table.)

7) Decorations: Choose decorations that will give your shower area a festive look. Include favors, name tags and place cards–they can help your guests get acquainted. Browse through floral centers, party, gift, and stationery and department stores, for ideas. Tell salespeople what you're planning and ask for their help (see our Decorations Guide, too).

8) Games: Plan your games and collect the equipment you'll need (pencils, paper, etc.). Purchase suitable prizes. There are shower game books in gift stores that contain not only

ideas, but actual game sheets for each guest. Look for our own *Games For Baby Shower Fun* book for the latest in shower games that are appropriate for women and couples.

9) Activities: Buy or make the props you'll need (for example, if you're planning a baby's memory book, have the questionaire sheets and pen available). Look over our Activities Guide for more ideas.

10) Plan or arrange any added attractions. If you're bringing in live entertainment, you'll need to clear your date with the people you hire. It's also wise to sign a simple, but specific contract. Select stereo music, special lighting, and other items beforehand. And look through our Added Attractions Guide for special touches.

11) Helpers: Contact guests you know well to help you run your shower smoothly.

12) Relax and enjoy!

Shower Planning Sheet

1) Guest List (Use separate sheet for additional names)

1_____

2_____

3_____

4_____

5_____

6_____

7_____

8_____

9_____

10_____

11_____

12_____

2) Date

   Time: From _____ To_____

3) Theme

   Special preparations needed _____

_____

4) Location _____

   Address _____ — ___

   Phone Number _____ Contract signed _____

5) Invitations Addressed _____ Mailed _____

   R.S.V.P. to _____ Phone _____

   Baby Registry at _____

   Gift type preference_____

6) Food (Also make a grocery list from your recipes)

Buffet _____ Sit-down _____

Menu:

Brunch _____ Luncheon _____ Dessert Only ___

_____ _____ _____

_____ _____ _____

_____ _____ _____

_____ _____ _____

_____ _____ _____

7) Decorations (Also make a separate list of items you must purchase)

Room _____

Serving Table _____

Gift-opening area _____

Special chair _____

Guest of honor _____

Guests_____

Order corsage for: _____

                Ordered _____

                Picked up _____

Helpers: _____

Favors (keepsake) _____

(Favors may also serve as name tags or place cards)

8) Games (if any):

1 _____

Prize _____

Equipment needed _____

_____

Game helpers _____

_____

2 _____

Prize _____

Equipment needed _____

_____

Game helpers _____

_____

(Helpers can give directions, distribute and collect equipment, create enthusiasm, and keep things moving.)

9) Activities (if any): _____

  1 _____

  Preparations _____

  _____

  Activities helpers _____

  _____

  2 _____

  Preparations _____

  _____

  Activities helpers _____

  _____

10) Added attractions (if any):

  1 _____

  Preparations _____

  _____

  2 _____

  Preparations _____

  _____

  Phone number _____

  Contract signed _____

  (Introduce performers before performance, and thank them afterwards)

Shower Protocol

As the shower giver, you'll naturally want to make your guests as comfortable as possible. Most often, all you need to do is be sure there's a way each person can meet others. You can do this either through personal introductions, name tags, or get-acquainted games and activities. If you also mention each guest's relationship to the guests-of-honor, you'll give your guests a "conversation starter" they'll appreciate.

Take the guest(s) of honor and let them know exactly what you've planned. It will help them in their role as guest(s) of honor.

Arrange a gift-opening area, and let the guest(s) of honor know when they should begin opening presents. Ask two helpers to sit on either side of the guest(s) of honor: one to keep gift and gift card together after opening, and to pass these around for guests to take a closer look; the other to gather the wrappings and to make a keepsake ribbon bouquet (see our Decorations Guide). Designate one other person to inconspicuously write down each gift and giver's name on a sheet of paper. This will make "thank-you-note time" much easier.

In a nutshell, if you concentrate on making others as comfortable as possible, nothing can go seriously wrong.

ShowerWise Guides

S howerWise and I looked at each other and realized
that this part had to be our greatest effort yet. We
didn't want you to miss ideas like our great baby bootee napkin fold, Cream Puff Pram recipe or chocolate kiss party favor from our shower themes. We also wanted to add other
party-making ideas as well. So off ShowerWise went to the
Great Baby Shower Galaxy Beyond the Milky Way. It wasn't
long—hardly an instant—and she was back with theme-
related decorations, sit-up-and-take-notice invitations,
anything-goes activities, and eye-catching recipes.

Take the time to look through this section and you'll be
sure to discover a special idea that will help make your shower a one-of-a-kind party. Everything is easy to find because
it's all put together for you in these eleven big guides.

Activities Guide

IDEAS FROM SHOWER THEMES

- Arrange a balloon-sculpturing demonstration and let the guests take part . . . as in Balloon Shower.
- Give everyone a chance to write good wishes for the baby on slips of paper and insert them into balloons. Blow up balloons and release the balloons all together in a grand finale . . . as in Balloon Shower,
- Ask your guests to share a part of themselves. Record their renditions of childhood lullaby songs or rhymes and present the tape to the new parents . . . as in Lullaby Time Shower.
- Invite the gang to get baby's nursery ready. Whether it's a complete paint job or a simple craft idea, the job will go much faster when good friends join together . . . as in Decorating Baby's Room Shower.
- Snip and mount nursery rhyme characters for the nursery walls . . . as in Another Idea following Decorating Baby's Room Shower.
- Make up a multiple-choice game of sun sign characteristics. Ask questions that will touch on the sun sign of each person who is playing the game . . . as in "Sun Sign" Shower.
- Videotape each guest with their gifts and good wishes as well as segments of the shower activities for the absent guest of honor who lives some distance away . . . as in Special Delivery Shower.
- Take plenty of instant photos during the shower. Slip them into the gift packages for the new parents . . . as in Another Idea following the Special Delivery Shower.
- Ask guests to fill index cards with how-to helps for child care. Decorate and personalize the cards with drawings, photos, magazine cutouts or fabric . . . as in Baby How-To Shower.

- Combine a word game with the opening of gifts. As the guest of honor opens a gift, she'll read a clue out loud. The correct answer must be given before the next gift can be opened . . . as in The "It's Twins!" Shower.
- Fashion a baby's quilt for the new mother . . . as in Quilting Bee Shower.
- Write down predictions of what the future will hold for the new baby in a small booklet . . . as in Quilting Bee Shower.
- Quilt a bumper pad, wall-hanging or playpen pad . . . as in Another Idea following Quilting Bee Shower.
- Give your guests textile marking pens and let them draw or write on a diaper-changing pad made of terry cloth washcloths . . . as in Another Idea following the Quilting Bee Shower
- Act out a jewelry heist mystery, and then spend time solving the mystery together . . . as in Solve the Mystery Shower.
- Ask your guests to guess how long it will take an ice block containing a baby bootee to melt . . . as in Next-To-New Shower.
- Stitch up a complete baby gift during the shower. Make it a group effort or an individual project . . . as in Baby Stitchery Shower.
- Present a program of speakers (friends of the guest of honor) who reminisce about moments in the new mom's life . . . as in Queen for a Day Shower.
- Play gift charades. The guest of honor acts out each syllable of the gift that she has just opened . . . as in Baby Registry Shower.
- Organize a lottery and encourage everyone to make a small bet on when baby arrives, whether it'll be a boy or girl, and the birth weight. Whoever makes the closest guess is the winner . . . as in Private Moments Shower.

- Sponsor a get-together cookie bake-off, and present the cookies to the new mom as unique and yummy shower gifts . . . as in the Cookie Bake Shower.
- Prepare casseroles as a group project. Everyone brings two or three basic ingredients and prepares the dishes at the shower . . . as in Another Idea following the Cookie Bake Shower.
- Conduct a diaper-changing lesson and contest. Any words of advice or tips from the guests will be welcome . . . as in the Disposable Shower.
- Invite guests to form teams and race to be first to finish a puzzle . . . as in the Puzzle Olympics Shower.
- Design a trivia game with questions galore about babies . . . as in Baby Trivia Shower.
- Fashion a memory book made of 8½ x 5½-inch paper with two punched holes at the top. Guests will answer questions on the paper designed to reveal fun and interesting things to know about baby's relatives. After everyone is done, collect the sheets, tie a narrow ribbon through the holes, and present to the parents . . . as in Family-Style Shower.

Invitations Guide

Printer-ready invitations can be found immediately following the Invitations Guide.

IDEAS FROM SHOWER THEMES

- Write formal invitations on white or cream-colored stationary . . . as in The Basic Shower.
- Send attention-grabbing invitations like singing telegrams or boxed baby bootees . . . as in The Basic Shower.

- Write an invitation on the label of nursery song records . . . as in Baby Brunch Shower.
- Divide the guest list so each co-hostess has no more than five to ten people to call . . . as in Second-Time-Around Shower.
- Send an invitation to a fictional event in a jewel heist mystery. Underneath add "You are REALLY cordially invited to a baby shower . . . as in Solve the Mystery Shower.
- Frame your invitations with adhesive photo corners stuck kitty-corner onto slightly larger sheets of paper . . . as in the Picture-Perfect Shower.
- Add a pinch of fairy dust (glitter) to the invitation envelope . . . as in Fairy Godmother Shower.
- Send off perfect-penmanship invitations on white or cream paper with a lace edging pasted on the edges . . . as in Victorian-Style Shower.
- Turn your invitation into a secret mission command . . . as in Mission-Possible Shower.
- Include the Chinese zodiac characteristics of the year in the invitation . . . as in Chinese New Year Shower.
- Invite your guests with homemade valentine notes . . . as in Valentine Shower.
- Type your invitation in the form of a want ad. Wanted: Guests with party experience . . . as in Next-To-New Shower.
- Use four-leaf-clover paper invitations . . . as in Luck-Of-The-Irish Shower.
- Create heavenly shower invitations with paper angels . . . as in The Littlest Angel Shower.

OTHER IDEAS

- Send a tiny plush animal with an inviting message tied to the ribbon around its neck.
- Plastic baby bottles (toy or the real kind) with a message tucked inside will sound the baby shower message loud and clear.

- Framed children's poems or cute sayings will highlight your invitation and set the mood for the shower.
- Issue a frosty invitation. Detail shower information with confectioner's sugar on a large lollipop.
- Record a small child's voice issuing an invitation to the shower. Send the cassette via mail or deliver personally.
- Print invitations on kites and tell your friends to "go fly a kite!"
- Buy cards with an appropriate photo or illustration on the cover and blank on the inside. Just script in our verse or your own.

Printer-Ready Invitations

If you use one of our printer-ready invitations, simply cut inside the broken line and have your local print shop reproduce as many copies as you need. You may purchase standard-sized envelopes there, or wherever stationery is sold. A good-quality copy machine may also be used to reproduce our invitations.

"SUN SIGN" SHOWER

Come to our "SUN SIGN" baby shower!

Baby's Sun Sign Is

Colors:

Flowers:

Gem:

For:

Date: Time:

Place:

Given By:

R.S.V.P.

P.S. Please give your month and day of birthday with your R.S.V.P.

Simply cut inside the broken line.

See Decorate Your Room Or Space for list of sun sign's flowers, colors, and gem.

"BEAR" NECESSITIES SHOWER

You're invited to a
"BEAR" NECESSITIES SHOWER!
Bear a gift . . . anything that reminds you of a cuddly bear!

For: _____

Date: _____ Time: _____

Place: _____

Given By: _____

R.S.V.P. _____

Simply cut inside the broken line.

OFFICE SHOWER

MEMO

TO: All Department Members

FROM: The Baby Shower Committee

SUBJECT: A VERY IMPORTANT TARGET DATE!

This memo takes precedence over all

other letters, reports, meetings, etc., etc.!

For: _____

Date: _____ Time _____

Place: _____

Simply cut inside the broken line.

"IT'S TWINS" SHOWER

IT'S TWINS!
Double the babies,
Double the fun,
We're having a shower,
So be sure to come!

For:

Date:

Place:

Given By:

R.S.V.P.

Time:

Simply cut inside the broken line.

LULLABY TIME SHOWER

You're invited to a
LULLABY TIME SHOWER!

Hey diddle diddle
Come with your fiddle.
We'll use a little time
To record a song or rhyme!

For: _____

Date: _____ Time: _____

Place: _____

Given By: _____

R.S.V.P. _____

Bring your favorite lullaby song or rhyme to record for baby's lullaby tape.

Simply cut inside the broken line.

Decorations Guide

DECORATE YOUR ROOM OR SPACE

IDEAS FROM SHOWER THEMES

- Tie balloons to the guest of honor's chair, stack them on the gift table and fasten them to light fixtures and drapery rods . . . as in Balloon Shower.
- Decorate your space with nursery rhyme characters . . . as in Lullaby Time Shower.
- String pink and blue ribbons or crepe paper across the room. Tape bows on picture frames or lampshades. Set small stuffed animals on the mantle, bookshelves, or small tables. Tie blue and pink ribbon around their necks and loosely twist the streamers around their legs. Tuck green Easter-basket grass under their feet . . . as in Baby Brunch Shower.
- Add visually to the shower theme with groupings of dolls and flowers. Prop baby dolls or Raggedy Ann dolls against the table lamp or back-to-back on the mantel or bookcase. Display cut flowers in children's play teapot sets and pencil boxes . . . as in Make-Ahead Shower.
- Hang the new baby's picture with a gorgeous ribbon and bow, or display photos in a small photo book on the gift table . . . as in Special Delivery Shower.
- At intervals through the room, arrange clusters of two balloons each tied together. Write the twins' names on the balloons . . . as in "It's Twins" Shower.
- Tack up a large banner outside the front door or garage announcing the arrival of the new baby or with information proclaiming a first-time grandmother . . . as in First-Time Grandmother's Shower.
- Roll out a red carpet (a long roll of paper will do) from the guest of honor's vehicle to the front door . . . as in Queen for a Day Shower.

- Tape up a garden gallery of baby pictures. Collect baby pictures of your guests and fit each picture into a paper flower . . . as in Family-Style Shower.

- Decorate your shower area with bear details. Set plush bears with armfuls of balloons in any available space and sprinkle illustrated storybooks of The Three Bears and Winnie the Pooh around the room . . . as in "Bear" Necessities Shower.
- Welcome the January baby with sparklers and the twelve animal signs of the Chinese zodiac . . . as in Chinese New Year Shower.
- Transform the shower area into a Cupid's retreat with red and white streamers, large and small bows, and red hearts everywhere . . . as in Valentine Shower.
- Scatter confetti and chocolate coins wrapped in gold paper everywhere . . . as in Mardi Gras Shower.
- Light up the night with candles – scented candles, floating candles, and tapered candles in potted plants . . . as in Midsummer Night Shower.
- Paste cherub wings to the baby's picture to introduce the newest littlest angel . . . as in The Littlest Angel Shower.
- Let baby's sun sign flowers, colors, and gemstones serve as a decorating guide. See the following list.

Sun Sign Gem, Flowers, And Colors List

ARIES
Gem: Diamond
Flowers: Star thistle, daisy, buttercup
Colors: Various shades of brilliant red

TAURUS
Gem: Emerald
Flowers: Daisy, goldenrod, violet, iris
Colors: Green, pink, yellow, red-orange

GEMINI
Gem: Agate
Flowers: Marigold, lily of the valley, gardenia
Colors: Blue, yellow, silver, green, white, brown

CANCER
Gem: Ruby
Flowers: Iris, lily, white rose
Colors: White, pale green

LEO
Gem: Sardonyx
Flowers: Poppy, peony, sunflower, red rose
Colors: Orange, amber

VIRGO
Gem: Sapphire
Flowers: Lavender, azalia, fern
Colors: Blue, gray-blue, yellow, fawn

LIBRA
Gem: Opal
Flowers: Violet, goldenrod, nasturtium
Colors: Bright blue, pastels

SCORPIO
Gem: Topaz
Flowers: Thistle, honeysuckle, anemone
Colors: Deep red, black

SAGITTARIUS
Gem: Turquoise
Flowers: Carnation, chrysanthemum
Colors: turquoise, purple, violet

CAPRICORN
Gem: Garnet
Flowers: Moss, ivy
Colors: Dark brown, deep green, black

AQUARIUS
Gem: Amethyst
Flowers: Daffodil, pansy
Colors: Violet, azure

PISCES
Gem: Aquamarine
Flowers: Tuberose, water lily, lily
Colors: Gray, green-blue, lavender

OTHER IDEAS
• Storks of all sizes
• Baby bootees as tiny flower vases
• Toy trains, wooden or plastic alphabet blocks, brightly colored balls, large decorater plastic pins
• Baby buggies (toy or antique)
• Colorful balloons (personalized or with a baby motif)
• Strings of plastic baby beads
• Opened umbrellas (paper, plastic, or fabric). Decorated with bows, streamers, flowers.
• Toy or plastic watering can with pastel-colored ribbons streaming from the spout.

DECORATE YOUR TABLE

IDEAS FROM SHOWER THEMES

- Make a visual impact. Arrange to have someone dressed as a stork to pour the coffee . . . as in The Basic Shower.
- Tie together a bunch of small medium-sized helium-filled balloons and tuck the end of the strings into a brightly colored bag. (The bag is going to be the anchor for the balloons.) Tuck tissue paper of a contrasting color into the bag around the balloon strings. Set the balloon centerpiece in the center of the table . . . as in Balloon Shower.

- Carry out the lullaby theme on the refreshment table with cutouts and a decorated cake of Mother Goose characters . . . as in Lullaby Time Shower.
- Spread a white tablecloth on the brunch table, and drape pink and blue ribbon lengthwise and crosswise on the table. Set a bowl of baby's breath in the center with tiny pink and blue satin bows tucked among the blossoms . . . as in Baby Brunch Shower.

- Pop a straw in baby bottles and use them as juice glasses . . . as in Baby Brunch Shower.
- Highlight a centerpiece of African violets with a small card saying "Libra's Preferred Flowers." Complete the decorative theme with ribbons and streamers in Libra's pastel colors . . . as in "Sun Sign" Shower.
- Serve Cream Puff Prams, a dessert sweet to see in teatable style. Choose decorative paper napkins with a motif that will complement the pram theme . . . as in Make-Ahead Shower.
- Dress up the table setting with this bright idea – a napkin baby bootee . . . as in Second-Time-Around Shower.

Baby Bootee Napkin Fold

Napkin Type: 15 inches square or larger, pastel colored, fabric or paper.

Directions:
1) Fold napkin into four parts to make a rectangular shape: Bring edge of napkin to center, fold again to the three-fourths mark and then fold to edge. (Start at edge closest to you and continue folding away from you. Don't turn over.)
2) Fold at "A" lines.
3) Bring A points to center by folding on dotted lines.
4) Fold it together, "B" on top of "B"towards you, with the smooth sides on the outside.
5) Turn napkin from pointing upwards to pointing to your left. This is the the toe of bootee. Make sure the opening of the toe is down and the fold line of the toe is on top.
6) There are two ends of the napkin on your right. Fold the end closest to you *behind itself* and up.
7) Take the second end, and fold down the portion "EE" at the dotted line.
8) Bring point "G" around and insert at point H. This makes the heel of the bootee.

9) Take edges of cuff and turn down around heel. Take the toe of the bootee and fold it in half underneath itself.

10) Put mints and nuts or a small spray of flowers in the opening and write guest's name on side of bootee.

Simply follow these diagrams.

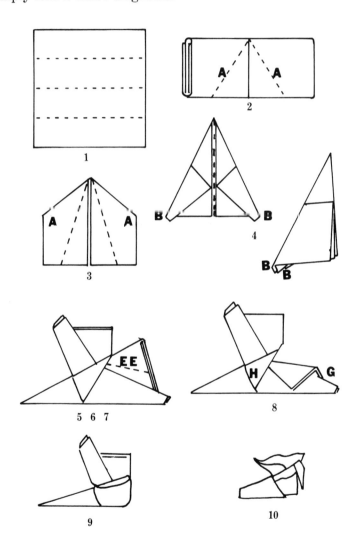

- Arrange groupings of wrapped presents with some flowers as a centerpiece at each small table or each section of a long banquet table . . . as in Second-Time-Around Shower.
- Make a special take-home centerpiece. Purchase a straw basket with a handle and spray paint in a pastel color. Line the basket with an appropriate baby patterned fabric and paint "For Baby" on the handle. Tuck a small wrapped present inside for each member of the family. The empty basket will make a handy decorative container for the nursery . . . as in Second-Time-Around Shower.
- Place two baby dolls in a small toy doll buggy for the centerpiece. Scatter daisies or carnations around the wheels of the buggy and write the babies' names on the buggy top. Tie a pretty bow with streamers to the buggy handle . . . as in the "It's Twins!" Shower.
- Fuss a little with paper ice cream cones for the centerpiece. Take 5-inch squares of brown wrapping paper and roll up diagonally from corner to corner (tape to hold together) to make the cone. Then top the cones off with "ice cream" (glue yellow and pink cosmetic balls to top of paper cone.) . . . as in Next-To-New Shower.

- Take a white lunch bag, trim it with sheeplike ears and "wool," and write the announcement of "NEW BA A ABY!" on the front . . . as in Bag a Lunch Shower.

New Baby Lunch Bag

Find white lunch bags at a party supply store or ask if you can buy a few white bags from your local bakery.

1) Use white construction paper. Cut out two ovals, each 2½ inches long, and fold lengthwise for the ears.
2) Round off corners at top of lunch bag as illustrated.
3) With the top edge of the bag folded over, draw black eyes and mouth on the folded section of the bag.
4) On the bottom section of the bag, print in large letters "NEW BA-A-ABY!"
5) Pack a light lunch in the bag, and tape the ears between the bag and foldover top on either side.
6) Paste white cosmetic balls or acrylic pom poms on the top edge of the fold-over section.

- Gather the tops of pastel-colored lunch bags together, tie tightly with a pretty ribbon,and add a baby rattle, diaper pins, or talcum powder bottle to the bow . . . as in Another Idea following the Bag a Lunch Shower.
- Feature the Flowerpot Dessert as an individual centerpiece . . . as in Queen for a Day Shower.
- Bake a bear centerpiece almost too lovable to eat . . . as in the "Bear" Necessities Shower.
- Wrap large white ribbon bows around the backs of chairs,and dress the table with a lace tablecloth or runner . . . as in Victorian-Style Shower.
- Decorate the refreshment table with crepe paper and paper roses to resemble Mardi Gras floats . . . as in Mardi Gras Shower.
- Carry out a spring theme with an artificial bird's-nest centerpiece and a bouquet of daffodils . . . as in "Hello Spring" Shower.
- Twist colorful streamers from a ribbon-wrapped cardboard maypole (cardboard wrapping-paper tube) to tiny baskets of flowers at each place setting . . . as in May Day Shower.
- Set an arrangement of spider mums on the refreshment table . . . as in Harvest Moon Shower.

OTHER IDEAS

Baby Sock Rosebud Centerpiece

3 pairs baby socks (pastel colors)
6 thin florist's wires
Florist's tape
3 potted house plants (fern, ivy, or philodendron)

To make a rosebud out of each sock, roll sock from toe to cuff. Roll the cuff down around part of the rolled up sock to form the outside rosebud petal. Insert a florist's wire into bottom of rosebud, and wrap florist's tape around the bottom of the sock and the wire. Tuck two rosebuds of different colors into each small pot of fern, ivy, or philodendron. The socks can be used later for the baby.

DECORATE YOUR GIFT-OPENING AREA

IDEAS FROM SHOWER THEMES

- Instead of one umbrella at the gift-opening area, use two tied together with a ribbon and bow. Underneath the umbrellas, lay two burping cloths with a little note saying "for the best-burped babies" . . . as in the "It's Twins!" Shower.

Burping Cloths
1) Add trim to plain cloth diapers.
2) Write the baby's name with a textile marking pen, or embroider name.

- Set a decorative carrier for the shower gifts in the gift-opening area. Find a used, oval clothes basket and pad the basket with a foam pillow covered with waterproof material. Slip a pillowcase around the foam pillow as a sheet for the pad. Finish off the basket by attaching bows, using the same color scheme as the pillowcase, around the rim. Set the bassinet on the gift table as a collecting spot for the other shower gifts . . . as in Next-To-New Shower.
- Make or buy a toy chest and decorate it to look like a treasure chest. Fill with gifts . . . as in Treasure Chest Shower.
- Decorate the gift table with crepe paper and paper roses to resemble Mardi Gras floats . . . as in Mardi Gras Shower.

- Wrap a large pot in gold foil and set it in front of a cardboard rainbow. As your guests arrive, stack the gifts casually in and around the pot . . . as in Luck-Of-The-Irish Shower.
- Feature a large cornucopia filled to overflowing with baby gifts . . . as in Harvest Moon Shower.
- Spiff up a child's toy buggy with satin bows and ribbons tied to the sides and handlebar. Line the inside of the buggy with a colorful baby blanket or quilt. As the guests arrive they can place their gifts in and around the buggy . . . as in Make-Ahead Shower.
- Make a ribbon bouquet keepsake out of all the ribbon ties from packages, after gifts have been opened . . . as in Shower Protocol.

Ribbon Bouquet Keepsake

1) Cut an "X" through the center of a paper plate
2) Draw ribbons of bows through the "X". Sick self-adhesive bows around the outer edge of the plate. When the entire plate is covered with bows, it resembles a bouquet.

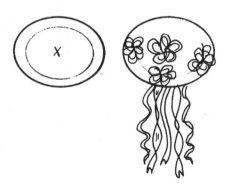

DECORATE YOUR SEAT(S) OF HONOR

- With ribbons, balloons, bows, tissue flowers, confetti, and crepe paper streamers, decorate a special chair for the guest of honor to sit in while opening gifts . . . as in Bag a Lunch Shower.
- Turn any available chair into a chair fit for royalty with a fake fur or purple fabric throw cover . . . as in Queen for a Day Shower.

DECORATE YOUR GUESTS

- Substitute baby bibs for napkins . . . as in Baby Brunch Shower.

Baby Bib

1) Turn one fringed end of a hand towel ½ inch over and tack down.
2) Run a ¼-inch-wide twill tape through the fold for the bib's tying strings.
3) Finish off the bib by writing each guest's name on the corner of the bib with a textile marking pen.

- Fashion masks – either hand-held or the kind secured around the head with a band – are de rigueur . . . as in Mardi Gras Shower.

DECORATE YOUR GUEST OF HONOR

- Set a gold crown on the guest of honor's head . . . as in Queen for a Day Shower.

Gold Paper Crown

1) Cut gold or yellow posterboard to fit around head as shown. Cut decorative points around top of crown.
2) Form a cylinder by rolling crown until ends meet. Tape tabs to inside.

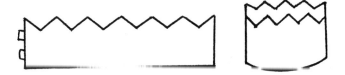

- Pin a bow or flower corsage with two pairs of bootees tacked to the center on the guest of honor . . . as in the "It's Twins" Shower.

Table Setup Guide

BUFFET BLUEPRINT

Serve a chicken and rice dish, vegetable salad, condiments, buttered rolls, beverage, and dessert. Arrange a miniature toy train set on the table with tiny vases of flowers scattered about.

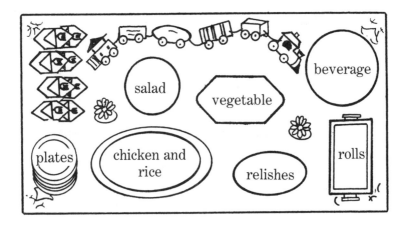

LUNCHEON BLUEPRINT

Serve a mixed fruit juice appetizer, quiche, green salad, hot rolls, beverage, and cookies for dessert. Decorate each table with the Baby Sock Rosebud Centerpiece (see Decorate Your Table).

DESSERT-ONLY BLUEPRINT

Serve a decorated baby shower cake, bars, chocolate candies personalized with baby's name, coffee, and tea. Choose flowers to match your theme colors.

Recipe Guide

IDEAS FROM SHOWER THEMES

TEDDY BEAR BREAD

. . . as in "Bear" Necessities Shower.
1 loaf frozen bread dough or favorite bread recipe
3 raisins
1 egg
1 ribbon for bow tie (blue or pink,) optional

Follow directions to raise bread, but don't put bread into a bread pan. Punch down and divide bread into four parts. Take two parts and shape together to form the body. Place on a well-greased cookie sheet. Use the third part to form the head; pinch head and body together securely. Out of the remaining part make two balls for the ears, four balls for the paws, and one tiny ball for the nose. Pinch on securely. Make indentations in the ears by pressing hard with your thumb. Put two raisins in the head for the eyes and one in the middle of the tummy. Beat together 1 tablespoon water and one egg; brush bear with this mixture. Bake at 375° F for 25 to 30 minutes. Bread is done when browned and tapping on the bread makes a hollow sound. Cool completely on a wire rack. Before serving, tie a ribbon around the bear's neck.

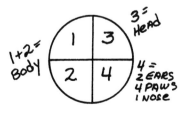

WISHING WELL

. . . as in May Day Shower.
1 large orange (one for each guest)
green grapes
cubed cantaloupe
any other fruit in season

Cut one-fourth off top of large, unpeeled orange and save. With serrated knife cut between shell and orange and between sections. Remove orange sections and save. Cut out remaining pulp. With a sharp knife, cut edge of orange into scallops. Cut a handle from a slice of the one-fourth section of the orange removed earlier. Cut fruit away from handle. Insert handle between scallops so you're sure it will stand upright. Spoon orange sections and other fruit into the well. Prop a paper umbrella on top of the fruit. Make one wishing well for each guest.

THREE LITTLE PIGS IN A BLANKET

. . . as in Baby Brunch Shower.
2 17.5-oz. cans refrigerator biscuits (20 biscuits)
6 5-oz. cans of Vienna sausage (30 sausages)

Heat oven to 450° F. Grease a jelly roll pan. Flatten one biscuit with your fingers so it is large enough to fit under three sausages side by side, with ½-inch extra on all sides. Place the sausages on the roll. Dab a little of your favorite mustard on each sausage. Flatten another roll to make the "blanket." Place the blanket on the sausage, but don't cover the heads of the "litle pigs." Pinch the other three sides of the flattened rolls. Bake at 450° F for about 6 minutes. Makes 10 servings.

CREAM PUFF PRAMS

. . . as in Make-Ahead Shower.
12 cream puffs (more oval than round) *
12 pipe cleaners **
48 semi-soft pastel mints
48 round toothpicks
12 1½-inch plastic baby dolls***

* Whipped cream makes a better 'blanket' than does custard filling.
** Available in grocery stores; choose the thin variety over the fuzzier kind.
*** Available in most craft stores; 1½ inches long, arms out-stretched, naked.

Purchase cream puffs from a bakery, or make from your own recipe. With a sharp knife, cut across the top of a cream puff, stopping about one-third from the end; remove, cut portion of top: discard (or, set aside to enjoy nibbling later). Sort mints by color, four per carriage (use mixed colors or all one color). Insert toothpick into flat underside of mint until tip protrudes out the other side for the "hub" of the wheel. (If inserted from rounded, top side of mint, hole will be too large and mint may fall off). Make four "wheels" in this manner, and insert other ends of toothpicks into the back and front of the pram, straight across from each other, to make four wheels. (The mints should just touch the puff.) Fold pipe cleaner to make a handle, and insert in cream in front portion. Wash plastic baby dolls (easiest to place in mesh bag and wash on top rack of dishwasher). Tuck cooled, clean dolls into the creamy coverlet. Serve on dessert plate on top of a paper doily.

FLOWERPOT DESSERT

. . . as in Queen for a Day Shower.

1 quart any flavor ice cream
12 chocolate sandwich cookies, crushed
6 chocolate sandwich cookies, whole
6 plastic drinking straws
6 new small clay flowerpots

Wash clay pots. Dry the pots and place one cookie at the bottom of the pots over the hole. Pack softened ice cream into each pot and sprinkle a layer of crushed cookie "dirt" on top. Stick a plastic straw in the center of the ice cream and push the straw down to the bottom. Cut off straw at the surface of the ice cream. Freeze the pots until shower time. Before guests arrive, set each pot on a paper doily and dessert plate. Tuck a flower in each straw and serve with cookies at the side of the dessert plate.

UMBRELLA SHOWER CAKE

. . . as in First-Time Grandmother's Shower
1 round layer cake
icing
sugar flowers

Cut off one-third of layer cake and reserve. Cut three V's from the remaining section, as shown. Cut handle from the reserved section and set into place. Frost. Draw "ribs" on the umbrella with contrasting icing and dot the umbrella with sugar flowers.

OTHER IDEAS

BABY BOOTEES

Stack three large-size marshmellows in a "L-shape as shown. Secure together with frosting. Fill in with stars, using a small decorater star tip and buttercream frosting. Pipe contrasting bow and small flowers on front of bootees. Great for cake tops.

WATERMELON BUGGY CENTERPIECE

Use a decorator tool or sharp knife and cut a zig-zag line as shown. For the buggy handle, use knife and cut end as shown. Cut away remaining rind and scoop out insides. Mix the insides with fruit salad. Carve handle from the end piece and anchor in place with toothpicks. Finally, slice a large orange into ½-inch thick slices and secure with toothpicks. Fill with fruit salad when ready to serve.

Favors, Name Tag And Place Card Guide

IDEAS FROM SHOWER THEMES

- Pass out balloon sculptures as a party favor to each guest at the balloon-sculpturing demonstration . . . as in Balloon Shower.
- Finish off baby bibs with each guest's name to be used as napkins as well as name tags . . . as in Baby Brunch Shower.
- Use sun sign pins to fasten name tags for a combined party favor/name tag . . . as in "Sun Sign" Shower.
- Set a napkin-fold bootee at each place setting. Tuck a tiny bouquet of dried flowers in the opening, and prop a name card against it for a party favor/place card . . . as in Second-Time-Around Shower.
- Buy pastel-colored pens and tie a ½-inch-wide white satin ribbon around the top half of each pen. In your best script or print, write "It's a girl!" or "It's a boy!" on the ends of the ribbon and add the birth date . . . as in Baby How-To Shower.
- Type or print this jingle on a paper buggy:

This chocolate kiss
Brings our best wish
For_____ and_____ (insert names of parents)
New Master or Miss!

- Tape a buggy to a foil-wrapped chocolate kiss . . . as in Office Shower.

- Decorate an In/Out office basket with pink and blue bows and fill with party favors . . . as in Office Shower.
- Purchase chocolate "cigars" with the name of the baby, or bake sugar cookies cut out into the shape of a little boy or girl. Decorate and write the baby's name with icing for a sugary party favor treat . . . as in the "It's Twins" Shower.
- Save your list of stitchery resources. It will serve as a favor to give your guests at the shower . . . as in Baby Stitchery Shower.
- Present a fresh or silk flower to each guest as a party favor . . . as in Queen for a Day Shower.
- Serve up tiny baskets of flowers for pretty take-home May basket favors . . . as in May Day Shower.

OTHER IDEAS

- Write name of guest with a felt-tip pen on baby rattle. Glue a large pin to rattle to secure as a name tag, or simply place the rattle on the table to serve as a place card.
- Use plastic duck, rabbit, etc., diaper pins to secure name tags.
- Stick a self-adhesive label to a baby bootee for a name tag or place card.
- Add drawings, fabric, buttons, borders, stickers, glitter, shells, or sequins to a white card, construction paper, or adhesive-backed label for tailor-made name tags or place cards.

Added Attractions Guide

IDEAS FROM SHOWER THEMES

- If you really want to see your guests get carried away, hire a hot-air balloon for rides . . . as in Another Idea following Balloon Shower.
- Rent a limousine, taxi, or horse-drawn carriage to bring the guest of honor to the shower . . . as in Queen for a Day Shower.
- Hire a color consultant to help your guests find colors that suit them best . . . as in Color Consultant Shower.
- Arrange to have a handwriting specialist give an analysis of each guest's handwriting . . . as in Handwriting Analysis Shower.
- Rent live background music for the shower. Set the mood with the soft sounds of a guitar, piano, violin, or harp . . . as in Midsummer Night Shower.

OTHER IDEAS

- Look in the Yellow Pages for entertaining acts, legal gambling setups and instructors, historical or scenic tours, singing telegrams, and in-person delivery of personalized messages.

Gift Guide

IDEAS FROM SHOWER THEMES

- Tie your gifts to a theme with printed or appliqué baby clothes, books, ceramic nursery lamps, pictures and prints for the nursery, mobiles, rugs, and music boxes . . . as in Balloon Shower, and "Bear" Necessities Shower.

- Grow charts, a baby scale, and a diaper pail are all welcome additions . . . as in Decorating Baby's Room Shower.
- Share helpful hints and ideas for bringing up baby on index cards. Organize them in a recipe box . . . as in Baby How-To Shower.
- Give hand-me-down family stuff or next-to-new items only . . . as in the Next-To-New Shower.
- Keep gift-giving simple with a baby's care caddy. Decorate a box or basket and ask guests to fill with baby powder, lotion, soap, shampoo, diapers, diaper pins and pacifier . . . as in First-Time Grandmother's Shower.
- Give fun gifts to the new grandmother, such as a baby photo album or a bumper sticker that says "Foxy Grandmother" . . . as in the First-Time Grandmother Shower.
- Highlight the new arrival and the coming together of two families with a family tree design . . . as in Family-Style Shower.
- Let the baby registry guide the gift giving . . . as in Baby Registry Shower.
- Turn the gifting to mother with hand-care products, books, magazines, bed jacket, and slippers . . . as in Private Moments Shower.
- For gifts that money can't buy, make up index cards as blank IOU's. Guests will fill them with promises of babysitting, a chili supper, or emergency consultations . . . as in "IOU" Shower.
- Cookie cutters spelling baby's name, a cake pan shaped as baby's first initial or a musical revolving birthday cake tray will solve baby's baking needs . . . as in Cookie Bake Shower.
- Plan gift giving around a special collection for baby . . . as in Collection Mania Shower.
- Shower the new mother with record-keeping supplies, such as a baby's album, medical records book, growth chart and babysitting emergency information . . . as in Setting-a-Record Shower.

- Picture the perfect gift – camera, film, albums, light meter, or video equipment . . . as in Picture-Perfect Shower.
- Pass on cherished family heirlooms or substitute "found" antiques . . . as in Heirloom Shower.
- Sports addicts would love an autographed ball from their favorite sports team for the new arrival . . . as in Pre-Game Shower.
- Fill out certificates good for sharing one personal skill with the child in the future. Anything goes, from fly-fishing to math tutoring . . . as in the Fairy Godmother Shower.
- You'll start a family tradition if you give a decoupage candle with baby's picture and birth information, to be used at subsequent birthday parties . . . as in Midsummer Night Shower.

OTHER IDEAS

- Elegant baby gifts: handmade hangers, fancy baby dresses imported from Brazil, handpainted nightshirts, picture frames, silver spoons, china baby shoes, musical pillows, burpy sets shaped to fit mother's shoulder, haircut boxes, tooth-fairy boxes, and silver toothbrushes.

Gift Wrap Guide

IDEAS FROM SHOWER THEMES

- Gift wrap with printed balloon paper and tie balloons instead of bows to the package . . . as in Balloon Shower.
- Make a puzzle out of a picture of the gift. Wrap the puzzle pieces as a gift and ask the new mother to solve the gift puzzle . . . as in Office Shower.
- Use a diaper bag or a decorated wastebasket as gift wrapping for several smaller gifts . . . as in Baby Stitchery Shower and Disposable Shower.

- Wrap up a gift in a designer diaper! Anything goes . . . decorated disposable diapers, flannel, lace, toweling, silk . . . just so it resembles a diaper . . . as in Designer Diaper Shower.

OTHER IDEAS

- Use grade schoolers' colorful artwork for a shower delight wrap-up.
- Tuck tiny gifts in a large seashell, a varnished walnut shell, or a small toy truck.
- Wrap large or bulky gifts in decorated garbage bags, paper tablecloths, large travel posters, nursery wallpaper prints, fabric drawstring sacks or an old pillowcase that's tie-dyed.
- Take a snapshot of a huge gift and wrap with directions to find the real thing.

Unusual Locations Guide

IDEAS FROM SHOWER THEMES

- Turn the tables and hold the shower at the guest of honor's home instead of your home . . . as in Decorating Baby's Room Shower.
- Give the second-time mom a night out at a favorite restaurant or country club . . . as in Second-Time-Around Shower.
- Shower the working mom at her desk, the conference room, or the cafeteria . . . as in the Office Shower.
- Bring the shower to your friends and their activities (locker room, church, or synagogue) . . . as in Bag a Lunch Shower.

- Whether you decide on your home, religious center, or community room, a shower will add to the happy memories of the new mother . . . as in Queen for a Day Shower.
- Send detailed instructions to an out-of-the-way location such as a park, beach area, or secluded cabin . . . as in Mission Possible Shower and "Shades of Campfire Days" Shower.
- Enjoy shower fun in your favorite sports arena parking lot . . . as in Pre-Game Shower.

Address Guide

IDEAS FROM SHOWER THEMES

- Baby Craft Companies . . . as in Baby Stitchery Shower. Bucilla, 150 Meadowland Parkway, NJ, 07094 Leisure Arts, P.O. Box 5595, Little Rock, AR 72215 Paragon Needlecraft, 5707 31st Ave, Woodside, NY, 11377 Patchwork n' Things, P.O. Box 3725, Granada Hills, CA 91344 Sunset Designs, P.O. Box 6698, Marietta, GA, 30063 Suzy's Critter Creations, 115 West Belair Ave, Aberdeen, MD 21001
- Brighton Publications, Inc., P.O. Box 12706, New Brighton, MN 55112 . . . as in Second-Time-Around Shower.
- Designing Women Unltd., 601 East Eighth St., El Dorado, AR 71730 . . . as in Baby Stitchery Shower.
- Maid of Scandinavia, 3244 Raleigh Ave, Minneapolis, MN 55416 . . . as in Baby Brunch Shower.
- Tree Toys, P.O. Box 492, Hinsdale, IL 60521 . . . as in Decorating Baby's Room Shower.

After the End . . .

P erhaps my expectations were limited. Somehow, as a home economist, I never expected to be working with a stork! That's not to say my experience with ShowerWise wasn't delightful. It was. As a matter of fact, I had such a good time writing this book that I'm hoping I'll have someone just like ShowerWise to help with the next book.

And, since I've brought up the idea of help . . . how about sharing any good ideas on wedding receptions, graduation parties, or birthday parties. I can't promise you your name in lights, but your name will appear with any selected helps or hints for fun and easy parties. Just drop me a line:

Sharon Dlugosch
c/o Brighton Publications, Inc.
P.O. Box 12706
New Brighton, MN 55112

For now, though, it's time to say . . . and this is from ShowerWise as well . . . we wish you the most successful, fun-filled baby shower of the year!

Shower Theme Index

Available from Brighton Publications, Inc.

Games for Baby Shower Fun by Sharon Dlugosch

Kid-Tastic Birthday Parties: The Complete Party Planner for Today's Kids by Jane Chase

Romantic At-Home Dinners: Sneaky Strategies for Couples with Kids by Nan Booth/Gary Fischler

Games for Party Fun by Sharon Dlugosch

Reunions for Fun-Loving Families by Nancy Funke Bagley

An Anniversary to Remember: Years One to Seventy-Five by Cynthia Lueck Sowden

Folding Table Napkins: A New Look at a Traditional Craft by Sharon Dlugosch

Table Setting Guide by Sharon Dlugosch

Tabletop Vignettes by Sharon Dlugosch

Games for Wedding Shower Fun by Sharon Dlugosch, Florence Nelson

Wedding Plans: 50 Unique Themes for the Wedding of Your Dreams by Sharon Dlugosch

Wedding Hints & Reminders by Sharon Dlugosch

Wedding Occasions: 101 New Party Themes for Wedding Showers, Rehearsal Dinners, Engagement Parties, and More! by Cynthia Lueck Sowden

Dream Weddings Do Come True: How to Plan a Stress-free Wedding by Cynthia Kreuger

Don't Slurp Your Soup: A Basic Guide to Business Etiquette by Betty Craig

Meeting Room Games: Getting Things Done in Committees by Nan Booth

Hit the Ground Running: Communicate Your Way to Business Success by Cynthia Kreuger

Installation Ceremonies for Every Group by Pat Hines

These books are available in selected stores and catalogs. If you're having trouble finding them in your area, send a self-addressed, stamped, business-size envelope and request ordering information from:

Brighton Publications, Inc.
P.O. Box 120706
St. Paul, MN 55112-0706

or call: 1-800-536-BOOK(2665)